the great
big book
of things to
make and do

the great
big book
of things to
make and **do**

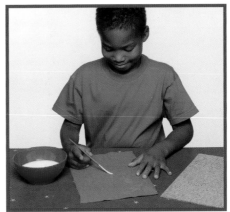

Cooking, painting, crafts, science, gardening, magic, music and having a party – simple and fun step-by-step projects for young children

HERMES
HOUSE

This edition is published by Hermes House, an imprint of Anness Publishing Ltd
Blaby Road, Wigston, Leicestershire LE18 4SE
Email: info@anness.com
Web: www.hermeshouse.com; www.annesspublishing.com

If you like the images in this book and would like to investigate
using them for publishing, promotions or advertising, please visit
our website www.practicalpictures.com for more information.

Publisher: Joanna Lorenz
Photographer: John Freeman
Designer: Peter Butler

ETHICAL TRADING POLICY

At Anness Publishing we believe that business should be conducted in an ethical and
ecologically sustainable way, with respect for the environment and a proper regard to the
replacement of the natural resources we employ.As a publisher, we use a lot of wood
pulp in high-quality paper for printing, and that wood commonly comes from spruce
trees. We are therefore currently growing more than 750,000 trees inthree Scottish
forest plantations: Berrymoss (130 hectares/320 acres), West Touxhill (125 hectares/
305 acres) and Deveron Forest (75 hectares/185 acres). The forests we manage contain
more than 3.5 times the number of trees employed each year in making paper for the
books we manufacture.

Because of this ongoing ecological investment programme, you, as our customer, can have
the pleasure and reassurance of knowing that a tree is being cultivated on your behalf to
naturally replace the materials used to make the book you are holding.

Our forestry programme is run in accordance with the UK Woodland Assurance Scheme
(UKWAS) and will be certified by the internationally recognized Forest Stewardship
Council (FSC). The FSC is a non-government organization dedicated to promoting
responsible management of the world's forests. Certification ensures forests are managed
in an environmentally sustainable and socially responsible way.

For further information about this scheme, go to www.annesspublishing.com/trees

A CIP catalogue record for this book is available from the British Library.

Also published as *The Ultimate Activity Book*

PUBLISHER'S NOTE

The level of adult supervision will depend on the ability and age of the child, but we
advise that adult supervision is always preferable and vital if the project calls for the
use of sharp knives or other utensils. Always keep potentially harmful tools well out
of the reach of young children.

Although the advice and information in this book are believed to be accurate and
true at the time of going to press, neither the authors nor the publisher can accept
any legal responsibility or liability for any errors or omissions that may have been
made nor for any inaccuracies nor for any loss, harm or injury that comes about
from following instructions or advice in this book.

Manufacturer: Anness Publishing Ltd,
Blaby Road, Wigston, Leicestershire LE18 4SE, England
For Product Tracking go to: www.annesspublishing.com/tracking
Batch: 0606-20571-0004

Contents

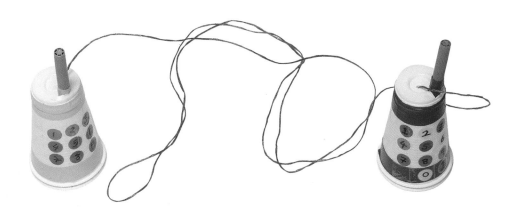

Introduction

If you've always wanted to make your own wrapping paper, grow your own strawberries, or put on a magic show, then this is the book for you. There are more than 100 exciting projects here, which you can do by following what the children in the photographs are doing.

Equipment and materials

All the projects in this book can be made easily at home. There are some basic pieces of equipment which you will need for many of the projects, such as scissors, glue and paints or felt-tipped pens. If you look after your basic equipment well it will last for a long time and you will be able to make lots and lots of the projects.

PVA glue

This glue has many other names. You may know it as white glue, school glue, or woodworking glue. It is water-based, which means that your hands and brushes come clean under the tap. It is white, so that you can see where you have put it, but it becomes clear when it dries, so any mistakes are invisible. PVA glue sticks most things together – wood, cardboard, paper, cloth and plastic. It is great for applying glitter too - just mix it in and paint it on. You can apply the glue with either a paintbrush or a glue spreader.

You can make a varnish by mixing PVA glue with water. Use three parts of PVA glue to one part water. Paint this on to clay flowerpots to make a waterproof surface to paint on. Papier-mâché used to be made with wallpaper paste, but this contains chemicals that can be harmful to your skin. A PVA glue and water mixture used with newspaper makes very strong papier-mâché and the glue can be used undiluted on parts that need extra strength.

Paints

There are lots of different kinds of paint, and it is important to use the sort that is best for the job you are doing. Sometimes pale watery colours are perfect and other times you need strong bright colours that will cover up printing or pictures on a recycled package.

The paint recommended for making most things is acrylic. It can be mixed with water, to make it runny, or used straight from the tube or pot to give a solid, bold

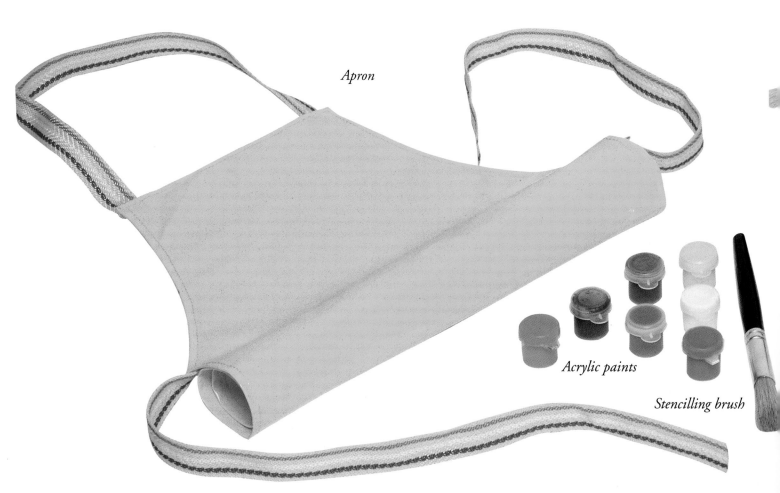

Apron

Acrylic paints

Stencilling brush

colour. You can wash your brush out under the tap, but you must remember to do it straight away, because acrylic paint dries very quickly, and brushes will spoil if they are not cleaned before the paint dries. Stand your brushes in a jar of water until you wash them out.

You can buy acrylic paints from stationery shops and art and craft shops where they also sell acrylic gloss varnish, used in some of the projects. There are many other kinds of paints available and you can find out more about them in the introduction to the painting chapter.

Paint pots
These are special paint pots with lids to stop you spilling the paint! They are very useful if you need to mix up a large amount of paint or to dilute paint with water. They come with lots of different coloured lids so you can match the colour of the paint to the lid. Always wash out the pots thoroughly before putting a different colour in them. If you are using undiluted paints in small amounts you can put them in a paint palette.

Paintbrushes
Paintbrushes come in many different shapes and sizes. Use thin, pointed brushes for painting fine lines and thick or flat-ended brushes for large areas. For stencilling you will need a short, fat brush with stiff hairs.

Take great care of your paintbrushes, and try not to damage them by being rough. If you move them in one direction this will keep them smooth and make them last longer. Always wash your brushes thoroughly after you have used them.

Apron
To prevent your clothes from getting covered in paint, wear a smock or an apron, or ask an adult for an old shirt. That way you can make as much mess as you like.

Ruler
This is useful for measuring and drawing straight lines.

Scissors
Scissors should not be too sharp and must be handled with safety in mind at all times. If you have to cut some thick cardboard and need sharper scissors, ask a grown-up to do the cutting for you.

Felt-tipped pens
Felt-tipped pens are always good to use on paper. The colours can't be mixed like paint, so it's best to use them separately.

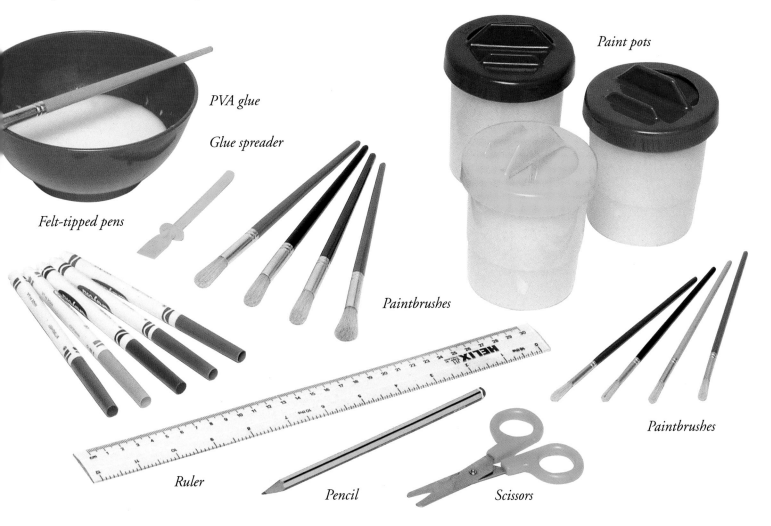

PVA glue

Glue spreader

Felt-tipped pens

Paint pots

Paintbrushes

Paintbrushes

Ruler

Pencil

Scissors

Sticky tapes
Masking tape is very useful because it does not stick permanently, like other kinds of plastic tape. You can use it to hold things together while the glue dries, and then remove it easily. You can get lots of brightly coloured sticky tape for decorating objects. Insulating tape, which electricians use, is ideal and comes in many widths.

Paper and card
Brightly coloured paper and card are fun and quick to use. But you can use white card and paper instead and decorate them in bright colours using paints, coloured stickers or felt-tipped pens.

Look out for lots of useful materials around the home.

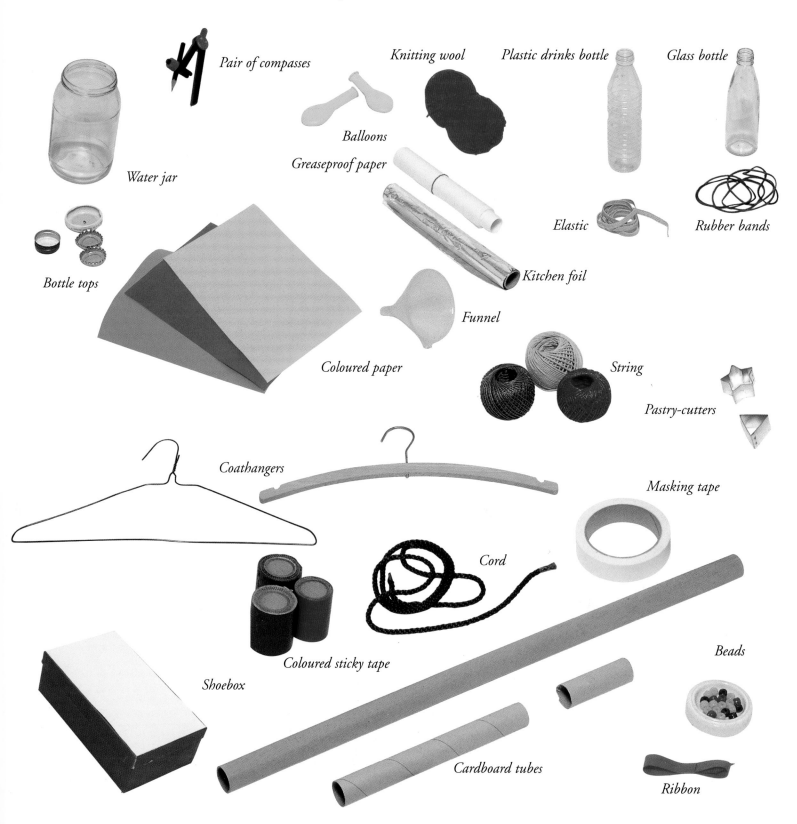

Pair of compasses

Knitting wool

Plastic drinks bottle

Glass bottle

Balloons

Water jar

Greaseproof paper

Elastic

Rubber bands

Bottle tops

Kitchen foil

Funnel

Coloured paper

String

Pastry-cutters

Coathangers

Masking tape

Cord

Coloured sticky tape

Beads

Shoebox

Cardboard tubes

Ribbon

Cutting Out a Circle

It is difficult to cut a circle out of thick card or cardboard. The best way to do it is to ask a grown-up to stab a small hole in the centre of the circle, using the point of a sharp pair of scissors. Make several small cuts outwards to the edge of the circle. You will now be able to cut around the edge of the circle quite easily.

Cut out towards the edge of the circle.   *Then carefully cut around the circle itself.*

Painting Straight Lines

Masking tape is very useful for this. Stick the tape along the line, then paint right up to it. You can paint a little over the edge. Wait for the paint to dry completely, then pull off the tape and you will have a perfectly straight line. This is a good way to paint shapes like triangles and diamonds.

Use masking tape to help paint straight lines.

Painting Plastic

To make paint stick to plastic surfaces, add the same amount of PVA glue as the amount of paint and stir well. If the mixture is too thick, add a little water.

Varnishing

PVA glue can also be used to make varnish, which will protect the surface of many of your projects. Mix the glue with one third the amount of water. The varnish will look a bit white when you paint it on, but when it dries it will be clear.

Mix PVA glue with water to make a varnish.

Painting Round Objects

It helps when painting an object, especially when it's curved, like an egg or a ball, to rest it in a holder. That way it won't roll around when it is drying. Plastic pots, mugs and egg boxes make excellent holders.

Round objects are easier to paint when they are propped up.

Templates

Some of the projects in this book have pattern templates for you to trace. You will find these on the following pages.

1 Place a sheet of tracing paper over the template pattern in the book. Hold the paper in position with your spare hand. Carefully trace the pattern using a soft pencil.

2 To transfer your pattern on to cardboard or paper, turn the tracing paper over and scribble over the outline with your pencil.

3 Turn the sheet of tracing paper over again and place it on your sheet of cardboard. Draw around the outline of the pattern firmly. It will transfer on to the paper or cardboard.

4 Remove the tracing paper and make sure all the pattern has been transferred. Use the scissors to cut out the template, and then draw around it as shown in the project pictures.

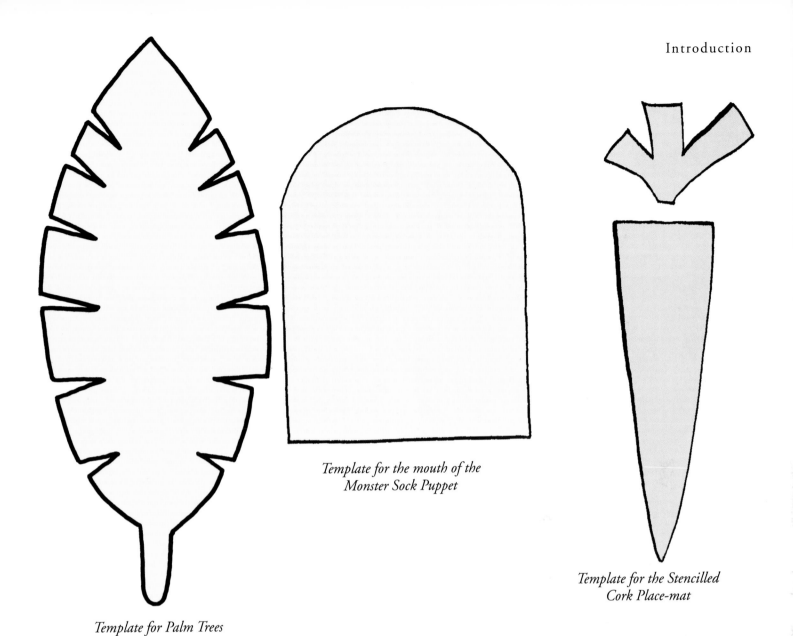

Template for Palm Trees

Template for the mouth of the
Monster Sock Puppet

Template for the Stencilled
Cork Place-mat

Stencils and circles

When you are making the stencil for the table-mat, trace the
template of the carrot from the book. Turn the tracing paper
over and scribble over the outline with a pencil, as shown in
step 2 on the opposite page. Turn the tracing paper over
again and place it on a piece of cardboard, but make sure
that it is in the middle of the cardboard. Draw around the
outline firmly, see step 3. Remove the tracing paper and go
over the outline to make sure the pattern is complete. To cut
out the stencil, make a hole in the middle of the design then
cut towards the outside edge. Move the scissors as you cut
the design. You want to end up with a piece of cardboard
with the pattern cut out of the middle. If you find it
difficult to cut the stencil then ask an adult to cut it using a
craft knife or some big scissors.

To draw circles, find a saucer, cup or any other round
object which is about the right size. Place the object on your
paper or cardboard and draw around it for a perfect circle.

11

Christmas Crackers

Flowery Glass

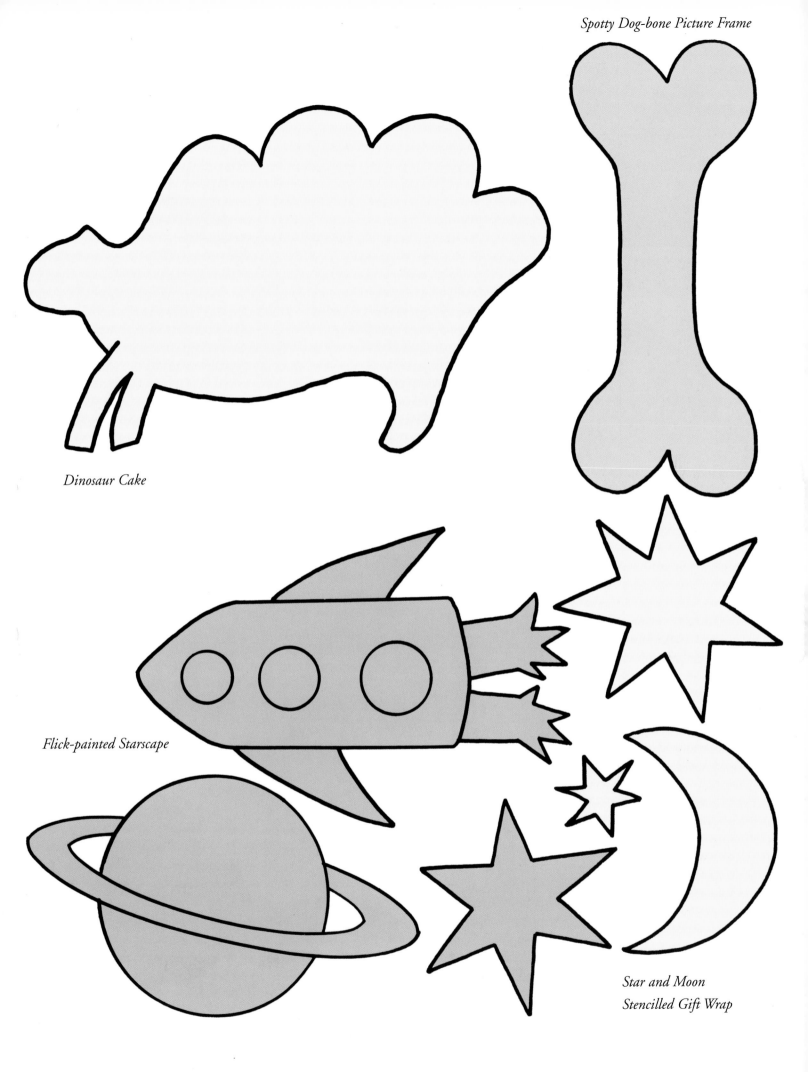

Spotty Dog-bone Picture Frame

Dinosaur Cake

Flick-painted Starscape

Star and Moon
Stencilled Gift Wrap

13

I Can Make Things

Introduction

Making things is great fun and very rewarding. It takes time and you have to concentrate to understand how things are put together. But all the hard work is worth it, because when you have made a rattlesnake or painted a flowerpot, it has some of your own very special magic in it. You will feel so proud, and everyone will admire your work. Once you understand how to make a mobile or cut flowers from felt, you will always know how it is done. Then you will be able to make up new designs of your own.

Look at the photographs of the children making up each project. They show you each stage and the words explain what they are doing. You can do it too, just follow what the children do.

Remember to ask a grown-up for permission before you begin making things. There are some projects that need a grown-up's help. Leave all the dangerous cutting-out to an adult, and never use a craft knife on your own as they are very dangerous. You may have to remind grown-ups that you are the one making things, because once they get started on the projects, they may not want to stop!

Be a crafty collector

We all like to recycle as much as possible. Once you start making things, you will be watching out to see what can be saved from the dustbin and made into a toy or a gift. You will need a good strong box for your collection and some-where to store it. If you save milk cartons and yogurt pots, give them a good wash in soapy water and dry them well, otherwise they may get smelly. Old tins and bottles are often

covered with labels which you will want to take off. The easiest way to do this is to fill a washing-up bowl with some warm water and soak the bottle in the water for approximately ten minutes. The label should peel off very easily. Collect small cardboard boxes and tubes, lollipop sticks, safe-edged tins, straws, corks, string, shells, bottle tops and cotton reels.

It is important to know when to stop collecting. If you have enough recycled packaging to fill your box, then start making things!

Colourful materials

For some projects you may have to use materials which you don't have at home, such as coloured card, felt, tissue paper, beads, pipe cleaners and wrapping paper. If you buy something special for a project then always keep any left-over scraps as they are bound to come in handy for any other project in the future.

Keeping clean

When you make things you can also make a lot of mess! It is most important to start off by protecting your work surface with old newspapers. Or putting down a tablecloth that will wipe clean. Do this first, because once you get involved with a project, it is easy not to notice the mess that you are making.

Wear an overall, apron or a big, old shirt to protect your clothes when you are painting. Before you start, roll up your sleeves as high as possible as they have a habit of dangling in paint pots and glue!

Getting started

When you have decided which projects you are going to make, collect together all the materials and equipment you will need and lay them out on your work surface. You will then find it much easier to work.

Clearing up

When you have finished, always clear up and put away all your things. Ask a grown-up to help you if you need to, but don't just leave a mess behind. Keep your equipment in good order and you will be ready to make something else another day.

Giant Sunflower Card

Sunflowers are among the tallest plants that we grow in our gardens, and this card takes its unusual shape from them. A sunflower has bright yellow petals and a big, rounded brown centre packed with seeds. This is the special part of the card that Kirsty is making.

This card would make a lovely present for Mother's Day, or a special gift for your teacher. Envelopes this shape may be difficult to find, so wrap up your card as a present. That is, if you can bear to part with it!

YOU WILL NEED THESE MATERIALS AND TOOLS

Large piece of blue card plus yellow, brown and green tissue paper

Needle and thread

Also a ruler, pencil, scissors, table knife, PVA glue, matchstick and a glue spreader

Tricky and sticky

The seed centre is the trickiest part of the sunflower to make, but once you understand how it is done, you will be making them all the time. The most important thing to remember is that too much glue will spread through the fine tissue paper and stick the next layer as well, and then the pop-up won't work. So use a tiny dot of glue, carefully pinching the two pieces of tissue paper between your finger and thumb to stick them together.

If you want to have leaves with jagged edges ask an adult to cut them out with pinking shears.

1 Cut out the card to 22 x 56 cm (8 ½ x 22 in). Find the middle, and score the card using a blunt table knife against a ruler. Just press firmly, so that the knife dents the card.

2 Fold the brown tissue paper over so that you have 10 layers. Cut out a circle that measures about 10 cm (4 in) across. Use a needle and thread to sew a running stitch down the centre line.

3 Cut out the petals, leaves and stems. You will need a lot of petals, about 30 to start with, two stems and five leaves.

4 To make the centre, think of a clockface. Imagine that the stitches go from 9 to 3. Using the matchstick, put a dot of glue at 12 o'clock.

5 Fold over the first layer of tissue and pinch it together where the dot of glue is.

6 Then, make two dots on the next layer of tissue. These go at where the 10 and 2 would be on the clock. Pinch together to stick. The next dot goes on the 12 spot and after that the 10 and the 2 again. Keep going like this until you reach the last layer. Let it dry.

Open up the card and there is your glorious sunflower.

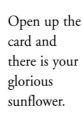

7 Draw a circle for the flower centre, and arrange the petals around it. Put a thin layer of glue on each one. Make two or three circles of petals.

8 Spread a stripe of glue down the centre line and stick the two stems on top of each other. Stick down the leaves and the flower centre in the circle.

Canal Boat

Canals are like roads made out of water. They were used to move all kinds of factory goods from one part of the country to another on long, low canal boats, called barges. A long time ago the canals were very busy, but now most factories use lorries or trains instead. People still use the canals and barges, but mostly as homes or for holidays. The barge people have always decorated their boats in the same way, using black, red, yellow and green paint. They would paint flowers and patterns on the barge itself and all their buckets, flower-pots, jugs and boxes. The skill of barge painting was passed down through families, and people took great pride in their painted boats.

YOU WILL NEED THESE MATERIALS AND TOOLS

 Tall milk or juice carton, with a pointed end

Pegs

 Cork

Bottle cap

Also scissors, ruler, pencil, black emulsion paint, white emulsion paint (optional), red acrylic paint, paintbrushes, PVA glue, strips of white paper 1 – 1.5 cm (about ½ in) wide, felt-tipped pens and acrylic varnish (optional)

Beautiful barges

Edward has decorated this barge in the traditional colours, but using felt-tipped pens to make the patterns. Every barge has a name, usually a pretty girl's name, like Jenny-Wren or Lindy-Lou. Choose a name for your canal boat.

1 Cut the carton in half lengthways. One half will be the boat. Cut off the ends of the other half, to leave a rectangle of card. This will be the roof of the barge.

2 To make the roof, measure 1.5 cm (about ½ in) either side of both the existing creases and score lines with a blunt pencil and ruler. The lines will make it easier to fold the card.

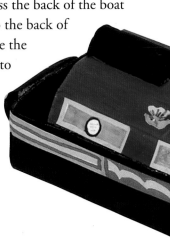

3 Paint the outside of the boat black and the inside too if you wish. The top can be painted white first. This will make the red much brighter. If not, just give the top two coats of red acrylic paint.

4 Fold the roof along the lines and glue the edges to the inner sides of the boat. Peg until the glue is dry.

7 Stick all the paper strip decorations to the boat with PVA glue. If you want to put the boat in water, give it a coat of acrylic varnish for protection.

5 Ask a grown-up to cut a cork in half lengthways. Paint the two halves black. When they are dry, glue one half across the back of the boat and one onto the back of the roof. Glue the bottle cap onto the front of the roof, as a funnel.

6 Decorate the paper strips with felt-tipped pens. Use red, yellow and green to make patterns, and write the name of your barge on the long strips if you wish. Draw windows and some flowers for the top, as bright and bold as you like.

A real work of recycled art.

Stencilled Cork Place-mat

Make this place-mat, and brighten up the dinner table, even before the food arrives. It looks so good that the whole family will want one, and you will have to make a matching set. Start by making one for yourself. Ephram has used a carrot design for his mat. He could make a set using different vegetable stencils for each mat.

Stencilling technique

Stencilling is great fun and easy to do if you remember two simple rules. Always hold the stencil firmly in place with your spare hand and never use too much paint on your brush. The paint needs to be thick, so don't mix any water with it. Dip your brush in and then dab it on a piece of kitchen paper before you stencil on the cork tile. Use a different brush for each colour.

The felt backing will protect the table surface and also strengthen the thin cork and stop it breaking if you bend it. If you like a glossy surface, finish off your mat with a coat of acrylic gloss varnish, or PVA glue and water mixed three parts to one. This will add a tough, wipe-clean surface to the mat.

YOU WILL NEED THESE MATERIALS AND TOOLS

Unsealed cork floor tile and orange felt

Pencil, tracing paper, card from a cereal box, to make your stencil and template

Also a ruler, craft knife, scissors, black marker pen (not watercolour), thick, soft stencil brush, acrylic paint – orange and green, kitchen paper towel, acrylic varnish, PVA glue and a paintbrush

1 Using a pencil and ruler, measure and draw a line about 10 cm (4 in) in from the cork tile edge. Ask a grown-up to cut this strip off for you with a craft knife.

2 Find the carrot stencil pattern in the introduction, trace it onto the card and cut it out. Use the scissors to make a hole in the middle of the design, and then cut towards the outside edge. Move the card towards the scissors as you cut.

3 Make a template of the zig-zag border from the card. It should be the same length as the long side of the mat. Use the black marker pen to draw around it and colour the shape in. Fill in the corners to make triangles.

4 Stencil the carrots, starting with the one in the middle. Work from the stencil card inwards towards the centre, using a light dabbing movement. Always dab the paint from the pot onto a kitchen paper towel before using the brush on the cork. Use the paint very sparingly. You can always go over it again to add more colour, but too much at first will make blobs. Wipe the back of your stencil before painting the next carrot. The paint will dry quickly, but wait until it has done so or you may smudge the pattern.

5 To protect the design, either coat it with a glossy acrylic varnish or a coat of PVA glue mixed with water, three parts to one.

7 Spread the felt with PVA. Make sure that you reach right up to the edges. Stick this to the back of the cork.

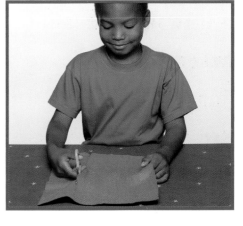

6 Cut the orange felt so that it is the same size as the mat.

More Stencilling Ideas

If you are more likely to eat your dinner from a tray, then you could paint it in the same way. If you have an old tray at home, ask whether you may decorate it. A wooden tray will need rubbing down with sandpaper first, and a tin tray may need a coat of gloss paint before you stencil it. You could use fabric paints to stencil onto plain dinner napkins, or just stencil paper ones with acrylic paint.

Butterfly Mobile

The butterflies in this mobile are made from mussel shells. You may not live near a beach where mussel shells can be collected, or have a garden where butterflies flutter about, but you can make this mobile that has a little bit of seaside and countryside in it.

If you have never tasted mussels before, this may be a chance to try them. Most fish-mongers sell mussels in their shells. When the mussels have been eaten, the shells are left, stuck together in the middle and already looking like butterflies. Scrub them well in warm soapy water.

YOU WILL NEED THESE MATERIALS AND TOOLS

7 mussel shells

Squeeze-on fabric paints, glitter, pearl or slick types

Gold paint and paintbrush

Pipe cleaners

Also 2 wooden boards, tin of paint for a weight, scissors, all-purpose clear adhesive, thin length of dowelling or garden cane, painted gold, and nylon thread

Fluttering in the breeze
Mobiles can be very relaxing to watch. Hang yours up above your bed and you will be able to drift off to sleep watching the butterflies gently turning in the air. Follow what Tania and Jade are doing and you will have a lovely mobile of fluttering butterflies.

1 Don't try to open out dry mussel shells, or they will come apart. Instead, soak the shells in warm water overnight. Open them out gently and place them face down on a board. Cover with another board and weigh it down with something heavy, such as a tin of paint.

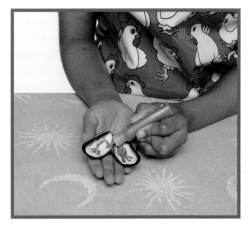

2 When the open shells have dried, decorate each one with a different pattern using the squeeze-on fabric paints. Practise on paper first to get the feel of squeezing the paint from the tubes. Look at pictures of butterflies – you will see how many different patterns you can use on your shell butterflies.

3 When the fabric paint is dry, turn the shells over and paint the dark side with gold paint.

4 Cut up a pipe cleaner to make butterfly bodies about 4 cm (1½ in) long. Use glue to stick them in place.

7 Seven very rare butterflies.

5 Put a drop of glue 1 cm (½ in) in from each end of the stick, then knot the nylon thread over one of the dots. The glue stops the thread from slipping, making the knot easier to tie. Measure roughly double the length of the stick and cut and knot the nylon onto the glue dot at the other end. This is what the mobile hangs from.

Butterflies Everywhere

It would be most unusual to buy just seven mussels from the fishmonger, so

you will probably have some left over. Decorate the shells with the paints and leave them to dry. Fix the bodies on as you did before and then glue them onto the corners of a picture frame or a mirror.

6 Put seven dots of glue along the stick, 6 cm (2½in) apart, and tie lengths of nylon over each dot. Tie the other ends of the nylon around the pipe-cleaner heads of each butterfly. Arrange them at different heights. It is very easy to tangle up the nylon threads so take care to keep each butterfly and its thread separate.

Feather Head-dress

YOU WILL NEED THESE
MATERIALS AND TOOLS

Piece of corrugated
cardboard

Beads

String

Pasta
quills

Pegs

Feathers,
large and
small

Elastic

Also scissors, ruler, white paper,
PVA glue and felt-tipped pens

The great Indian chiefs of North America wore head-dresses made from eagle feathers. They painted the feathers with patterns and each one had a special meaning, telling people how brave they were and how many battles they had won. Some chiefs wore head-dresses that reached all the way down their backs, from head to feet, called trailer war bonnets. When they held important gatherings or fought wars between the tribes, they would wear their feathers to show how brave and fierce they were. All the tribes understood the meaning of the feathers.

Magic feathers

Thomas and Edward are making this feather head-dress from seagull feathers, pasta quills, corrugated cardboard, beads and string. You can use any large feathers, so keep a look out when you go for a walk in the park or by the sea. If you live near a farm you can collect chicken or duck feathers.

Medicine men wore their feather head-dresses when they used their special powers, so perhaps you could wear yours and do a rain dance or, even better, a sunshine dance!

26

1 Cut the corrugated cardboard into a strip 4 cm x 25 cm (½ x 10 in) and two discs 6 cm (2½) across. Cut white paper to match.

2 Glue the paper to the cardboard strip. Draw the beadwork pattern onto it with felt-tipped pens.

3 Glue the two paper discs to the cardboard discs. Decorate them with beadwork patterns.

4 Cut two lengths of string 18 cm (7 in) long. Thread beads onto each end of the string and make a knot below them.

5 Dip the end of a small feather in the glue and use it to push the middle of the string up into a channel in the corrugated card disc. This is quite fiddly so ask a grown-up for help if you find it difficult.

6 Place a pasta quill on each large feather and push the ends down into the channels in the decorated cardboard strip. Arrange the biggest ones in the centre, using smaller ones towards each side.

7 Glue on the discs about 2.5 cm (1 in) from each end. Peg the pieces together until the glue has dried. Make a hole at each end of the strip and thread elastic through to fasten at the back.

Beautiful Beadwork

The North American Indians made wonderful clothes and jewellery from beads, feathers and strips of leather. They believed that every living thing on Earth was precious and many of the patterns they used for beadwork or weaving told stories of nature and the lives of their ancestors. Ask at your library for a book about them, and copy the beadwork patterns to make pictures using felt-tipped pens or crayons. Try making jewellery from strips of chamois leather (we use it for car washing) threaded with beads and tubes of pasta, like macaroni. And don't forget to do that sunshine dance!

Jewellery Box

YOU WILL NEED THESE MATERIALS AND TOOLS

Plastic box with a hinged lid

Felt squares and scraps   Fabric paint and a paintbrush

Also thin paper, to make templates, pencil, pins, scissors, pinking shears (optional), PVA glue and a glue spreader

Some packaging is just too good to throw away. If you have a baby sister or brother, there may be some empty "wet wipes" boxes which have hinged lids and a clasp to keep them shut. You can decorate them with pieces of felt and make a very special box to keep your jewellery in. Felt is easy to cut, and craft shops sell squares 30 x 30 cm (12 x 12 in) as well as small bags of scraps in different colours.

The zig-zag edge is made by using special scissors called pinking shears. Dressmakers use them, so ask a grown-up who you know does a lot of sewing if they have a pair you can borrow. Felt is such fun to cut out anyway, so if you don't have pinking shears just cut your own fancy edges with scissors.

This box belongs to …
Everyone has favourite colours, so choose the ones you like best when you cover the box. Fabric paints come in all colours and are either pearly, puffy or shiny when they dry. You will need to practise writing to avoid making blobs. Kirsty is making a box for her friend Maria. You could write your name instead. Try it out a few times on different pieces of felt, and choose your best effort to stick on the box.

1 Make paper templates by drawing around the top, long and short sides of the box. Cut them out, but make the patterns a bit smaller if your box has raised edges like this one.

2 Use pins to hold the patterns and felt pieces together. Choose different colours of felt for the top and sides of the box.

3 Cut out the felt pieces. Use pinking shears if you have them, or ordinary scissors if not. If you use pinking shears ask a grown-up to cut out the pieces of felt for you.

4 Stick the felt to the top and all the sides of the box.

5 Cut out circles of felt, about 4 cm (1½ in) across for the flowers, and smaller ones for the flower centres. Stick the centres down and snip towards the centre to make petals. Cut out some flower stems too.

6 Glue the flowers to the top and sides of the box.

Fun with Felt

If you enjoy snipping and gluing felt you could make a cover for your diary or a folder. Measure the shape and cut the background coloured felt to fit. Cut out shapes and patterns, letters and numbers, and glue them onto the background. Always make sure that the glue is spread evenly across the felt and right up to the edges.

Felt can be used on its own to make things too. A bookmark is useful. Just cut a long strip and snip 1 cm (½ in) into the ends to make a fringe.

7 Using a paintbrush, write your name on a piece of felt with fabric paint. Try writing in small dots if lines seem too difficult.

Now that you have made it, you will probably need some new pieces of jewellery to go in your jewellery box!

Painted Flower-pot and Saucer

Everyone loves a gift that has been specially made for them. You may not be ready to make a flowerpot yet, but you could certainly decorate one as a special present.

Indoor plants can look dull in plain clay pots, especially the leafy ones without any flowers. This bright red and yellow pattern that Roxy is painting is very easy to do and is just the thing to brighten up a winter windowsill.

Preparing your pots

Clay pots need to be sealed before you can paint them, and PVA glue can be brushed on to give a good waterproof paint surface. When you paint stripes around a shape like a flowerpot, it is hard to keep the lines straight. A good trick is to put a rubber band around the pot wherever you need a guideline. It makes a slightly raised line to paint up to and can be slipped off when the paint is dry.

YOU WILL NEED THESE MATERIALS AND TOOLS

Houseplant

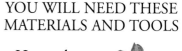

Clay flowerpot and saucer

Also PVA glue, to seal the surface of the pot, paintbrushes, acrylic paint – red and yellow, and a rubber band

1 Mix up three parts PVA glue with one part water and brush this all over the flowerpot and the saucer. Leave them to dry.

2 Paint the outside of the flowerpot and its inner rim and the outside of the saucer yellow. Mix acrylic paint with a little water, to make it thick and creamy. Leave it to dry and then paint on a second coat.

3 Stretch a rubber band around the flowerpot to mark the edge of the red section. Paint as shown in the picture. Leave the rubber band on until the paint is dry.

4 Make two red stripes with dots in-between them around the outer rim of the pot.

5 Paint the rim of the saucer red. Allow to dry. Then decorate the saucer with red spots on the yellow background and yellow spots on the red background.

6 Make yellow dots along the red stripes at the top of the pot. Paint yellow stripes down to the bottom edge, over the red. Paint big red dots in the middle and, when dry, put in smaller yellow dots. When all the paint has dried, seal the pot with the same PVA glue and water mixture that you started with in the first step.

A little bit of sunshine to put on the windowsill.

Go Potty Painting Pots!

Flowerpots come in all sizes and there are many different ways to paint them. Spots, stripes, wavy lines, diamonds, flowers – these are a few of the different shapes that you could use to make patterns. Stars look great too. Try making a stencil out of a piece of card. Cut out the shape with scissors and hold it firmly against the pot. Paint through the stencil, being careful to use only a tiny amount of paint on your brush.

Cork Rattlesnake

This cork and bead snake has a slithery feeling and will curl up or wriggle along, just like the real thing. Rattlesnakes get their name from the rattle at the end of their tail. They curl up and shake the rattle, holding their heads ready to strike when danger approaches. The rattling sound warns all creatures to beware as the rattlesnake is very dangerous.

YOU WILL NEED THESE MATERIALS AND TOOLS

10 winemaker's bored corks
Coloured beads – large-holed
60 cm (24 in) of flat elastic 1–1.5 cm (about ½ in) wide
Pipe cleaner
Rubber bands
Also paintbrushes, acrylic paints – green, black, red and yellow, ordinary cork, cut in half lengthways, PVA glue, scissors and acrylic varnish (optional)

Colourful crazy patterns

The corks used in this project have holes through the middle and are usually used for making home-made wines. You can buy them from large chemists and shops that specialize in winemaking equipment. Ordinary corks could be used, but you would have to ask an adult to drill holes through the middle of them for you.

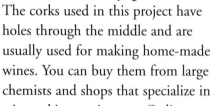

Snake colours are brilliant and their patterns are exciting. Zig-zags, diamonds, stripes, swirls and spots are all very snaky. Look at what Reece and George have done and then have fun with your patterns and make a really unusual rattlesnake.

1 Paint all the corks green. Leave them to dry completely.

2 Paint the black pattern first. Then paint the red and yellow patterns in-between the black ones. Don't forget to decorate the ordinary cork that has been cut in half. This will be made into the mouth.

3 When the paint is dry thread the main body of the snake onto the elastic, with a bead between each cork. The corks are thicker at one end than the other. Make sure the tail cork tapers to the thin end.

4 Thread five or six beads onto the end of the snake to make the rattle. Tie a knot at the end.

7 Cut the elastic into the shape of a forked tongue and paint red. The snake can be varnished with acrylic gloss or PVA glue diluted with water.

5 Pull the elastic up through the snake. Don't pull it too tight though, because the snake must be able to wriggle and roll up. Thread two beads onto the pipe cleaner to make the snake's eyes. Cut off the extra pipe cleaner leaving 1 cm (½ in) to twist and secure the beads in place. Flatten out the elastic so it runs along the flat side of the cork and sticks out at the end. Place the pipe cleaner across the elastic.

A slithery snake pet with no nasty nips.

6 Paste with PVA glue and put the other half of the cork on top. Hold the two pieces together with a rubber band until the glue is dry.

Slithery Lizard

You could make a lizard out of corks. For the legs, ask a grown-up to make holes across two of the corks. Make the lizard up in the same way as the snake, then thread shorter pieces of elastic through the new holes. Thread three beads on each side and then a cork, with the wide end down. Add one more bead and tie a knot. Four corks added in this way will make four stubby lizard legs.

Doll's House

The next time you visit a supermarket, choose a good strong cardboard box from the check-out to use to pack the shopping. When the groceries are all put away, you can use the box to make this doll's house.

You will need a grown-up to help with the first stages. Never use a craft knife on your own as the blades are dangerously sharp. The step photographs show how the box is cut, and you can help with a ruler and pencil, measuring and drawing the cutting guidelines, just as Kirsty is doing here.

Paint the house and roof with a light-coloured emulsion paint, the sort that is used to paint walls at home. This will make a good base coat for felt-tipped pens.

YOU WILL NEED THESE MATERIALS AND TOOLS

Sturdy cardboard box

Corrugated cardboard

Also light-coloured emulsion paint, paintbrushes, pencil, ruler, scissors, craft knife, adhesive tape, table knife, PVA glue, acrylic paints – red , yellow, and blue, paper, and felt-tipped pens

Moving in
This house is empty, and will need furnishing. Look for little boxes and tins to cover with fabric or felt as they will make good chairs. A carpet sample could be cut to fit inside, or you could colour paper to make a patterned rug. And to make the house your very own, you could write your house number on the door.

1 Paint the box. On both sides measure 10cm (4in) from the top. Find the middle point along the top edge. Join the dots and draw a triangle.

2 Ask a grown-up to cut out the shape of the house for you using big scissors or a craft knife.

3 The back of the house should be cut away so you can reach inside. Ask a grown-up to do this with the craft knife.

4 Use the side flaps to create the roof peak. Score the lines where they fold but don't cut right through. Stick the flaps down with adhesive tape.

5 To make the roof, measure the top of the box. Cut the corrugated cardboard so it is 2.5 cm (1 in) wider each side and 5 cm (2 in) longer at each end. Score down the central line with a table knife. Ask a grown-up to help you if you need to.

6 Bend the roof along the scored line. Paint the inside with PVA glue and place it on top of the house. When the glue is dry, paint the roof with yellow acrylic paint.

Budding Architect

You could make lots of different buildings out of cardboard boxes. Perhaps you would like a garage to go with your house. You could even make a whole street of different buildings, including shops and a church.

Look for different sized boxes, such as shoe boxes, and other things. What could you use to make a post box, for example?

7 To make the windows, cut out squares of paper and paint the edges with blue acrylic paint. Cut out a front door and paint it red.

A pretty country house complete with cat, ready to be moved into and furnished.

Birdwatchers

If you have ever seen birdwatchers, you'll have noticed that they are very quiet and slow-moving. Any sharp movements or noises would frighten the birds and they would fly away.

These binoculars are green so they are camouflaged as you creep around the park or garden birdwatching. Stay very still and the birds will come quite close. If you have a bird-bath or table in your garden, the birds that use it will be quite tame, so they might not mind even if they do see you watching.

Sunny all the time

These binoculars have a very special feature. They brighten up dull days, making the world outside look sunny, even when it's grey. George has found some sweets with yellow cellophane wrappers – just the thing to cover the ends of his binoculars.

YOU WILL NEED THESE
MATERIALS AND TOOLS

Two toilet-roll tubes

Green paper,
ruler and pencil

Piece of yellow
cellophane

Adhesive tape

Black plastic tape
Black cord

Also scissors, a wine cork, PVA glue, paintbrush, black acrylic paint and a rubber band

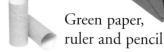

1 Cut out two squares of cellophane and tape them over one end of each cardboard tube. Ask a grown-up to help if you find this difficult.

2 Cut out two rectangles of green paper measuring 12 x 19 cm (4½ x 7½ in). Then cut a strip of paper to fit around the cork.

3 Ask a grown-up to trim the cork lengthways, so that one half has two flat sides. Paint the ends with black acrylic paint.

4 Take the strip of green paper and glue it around the cork. Paint on lines for the focusing winder.

5 Brush the pieces of green paper with glue. Line up with the tube ends without cellophane, then roll the tubes onto the paper.

6 Stick black plastic tape around the ends with the cellophane, then trim the paper and tape close to the cellophane ends.

7 Spread a stripe of glue along the side of one tube, and both flat sides of the cork. Assemble the binoculars, and hold them together with a rubber band until the glue is dry.

8 Push a hole through the sides of each tube, and thread the black cord through. Tie a knot on the inside.

Now you are ready to go birdwatching – and the weather looks just fine!

41

Monster Sock Puppet

Everyone has an odd sock somewhere around the house, waiting to be brought to life as a monster sock puppet. Try to find one that is brightly coloured and use a con-trasting colour felt for the mouth and fins. Kirsty has practised her monster noises, because she is going to need them!

Pins and needles

If you have never used a sewing needle before, be sure to ask a grown-up to help you. Sewing is quite easy, once you know how, and you will not need to use a very sharp needle to sew through felt and sock material. A darning needle will do the job.

If you use pins to hold the mouth lin-ing in place as you sew it, be very care-ful, because they are sharp. Always position them so their points are facing in the same direction around the mon-ster's mouth. When you start to sew, work towards the heads, not the points, of the pins. Each time you reach a pin, remove it and put it back in a pin cushion or tin, so that nobody gets a sharp surprise!

YOU WILL NEED THESE MATE-RIALS AND TOOLS

Plain coloured sock

Felt, different colour from the sock

Darning wool and needle

Two large buttons

Also a pencil, tracing paper, paper, scissors, pins (optional), thread, PVA glue and a glue spreader

1 Trace the template for the mouth which you will find in the introduction. Cut it out to make a pattern. Put this on a folded piece of felt, so that the fold is along the straight edge of the pattern. Cut out the mouth and the other shapes. Just nip the felt to make zig-zags, spiky fins, and a tongue.

2 Turn the sock inside-out and cut along the toe seam and past it on both sides by about 5 cm (2 in). Measure the opening against the pattern for the mouth, to get the size right.

3 Pin the mouth lining into the toe end, flapping the top back, so that you can sew the lining in one flat piece. Sew along the seam using running stitches. Make a small cut along the fold of the mouth and poke the tongue through it, so that it sticks out on the other side. Sew the tongue in place.

4 Turn the sock right side out and sew on buttons or eyes. Use wool to do this, pushing the needle up from inside the sock, through the holes and back down again. Tie the ends of wool inside the sock.

5 Stick on the nostrils, spreading PVA glue across the back of the felt, right up to the edges. Stick on the triangles and zig-zags in the same way.

6 Sew the long back fin along the centre of the monster's back, using black thread or wool. Be careful not to prick your hand with the needle.

Now is the time to use those monster noises that you have been practising!

Shark Alert!

There are all kinds of creatures to be made from odd socks. If you have a grey sock you could try making a shark. You will need grey felt for the fins and red for the mouth lining. Nice white teeth are a very important feature, so cut them from felt and fit them into the mouth at the same time as the lining. Think carefully as they will need to stick up from the shark's gums. So cut triangles and sew the flat ends into the mouth seam, leaving the pointy teeth to stick up in the mouth. To make the big back fin, cut two triangles and put a bit of cotton wool stuffing in-between them. Sew around the edges and then sew the base of the fin into the middle of the back.

I Can Cook

Be Clean and Tidy

When you are cooking and handling food, you must be aware of the bacteria which are all around. Most bacteria are harmless, but it is important to keep the harmful ones away by following a few simple rules.

❖ Always wash your hands before you handle food and keep washing them every now and then while you are cooking, to keep them as clean as possible.

❖ Wear a clean apron and tie long hair back.

❖ Have a clean, damp cloth handy, so you can wipe the surfaces if you make a mess. Don't forget to rinse the cloth when you have used it.

Wash your hands before you start to cook and dry them on a clean dish towel.

❖ Try to tidy up and wash up as you go, so you won't have so much to do at the end.

❖ Wash your chopping board regularly and every time you use it for a new ingredient.

❖ Always wash fruit and vegetables before you use them and clear away any peelings.

❖ Have a rubbish bin near by, so you can keep putting things in it rather than letting the rubbish pile up as you cook.

Be Safe in the Kitchen

There are some things in the kitchen which can be very dangerous. Make sure you have a grown-up's permission before you start cooking and ask them to be around to help with the more dangerous stages of cooking. Always read through the recipe to see when and where you might need the help of a grown-up, then follow these basic rules:

❖ Always ask a grown-up to light the oven or stove top – never do it yourself.

❖ Go slowly and carefully in the kitchen – rushing around causes accidents.

❖ Always use oven gloves or a dish towel when handling hot things. Better still, ask a grown-up to do it for you.

❖ Never leave the kitchen when something is cooking – you don't know what might happen while you're gone!

Always wear an apron to protect your clothes when cooking.

Place hot bowls or saucepans on a trivet to protect the work surface, and use oven gloves or a dish towel to hold hot things.

❖ Make sure you turn saucepan or frying pan handles to the sides of the cooker when they're on the stove top. This will stop you knocking or catching yourself on them.

❖ Never touch electrical equipment, plugs, sockets or switches when your hands are wet. You might get an electric shock.

❖ Take great care when using sharp knives. Chop on a chopping board and point the knife downwards. Keep all your fingers well out of the way.

❖ Stand away from frying food or boiling water. Always ask a grown-up to do these stages for you.

❖ If you spill anything on the floor while you are cooking, wipe it up straight away, otherwise you might forget it's there and have a nasty accident later.

❖ It's a good idea to have a heatproof mat or trivet handy on the table to put hot pans straight on to.

Always use a chopping board when cutting things and keep your fingers away from the knife.

Preparing Vegetables

Most vegetables need washing and peeling before you can use them in your recipes. Some need chopping or slicing. It might be safer to get a grown-up to do this for you. If you can do it yourself, here are some common vegetables and ways to prepare them for use.

Slicing and chopping an onion To slice the onion in half, put the flat side on the chopping board and slice across the onion from side to side. If you want to chop it, try to keep the slices together and slice down from the top to the bottom.

Shredding carrot Grate a carrot through the biggest holes on the grater. Or, with the help of a grown-up, you can do it in the food processor.

Shredding lettuce Use a crunchy lettuce such as an Iceberg. Remove the outer leaves and then cut the lettuce in half from the top to the bottom. Lay the flat side on your chopping board and cut across at about 12 mm (½ in) intervals. This will give you ribbon strips of varying lengths.

Cucumber slices and strips Cut a length from the cucumber and peel it with a vegetable peeler if you like. Cut it in half lengthways. Put the flat side on your board. For slices, cut across the half as finely as you can. For strips, cut the cucumber half lengthways into three thick slices and then cut each slice from top to bottom into long strips.

Cut an onion in half, peel off the skin and then slice or chop it carefully with a sharp knife.

Peel carrots with a vegetable peeler before you grate them.

Glossary

Here are some cookery words and their meanings that are used in the recipes. These will help to help make things clearer when you are following the instructions.

Beat Mix ingredients together very hard, stirring with a wooden spoon.

Boil Cook at a high heat on the stove top until the water or food bubbles fast.

Garnish Add a decoration to savoury food, to make it look more attractive.

Grease Cover baking tins or trays with a light layer of butter, margarine or oil to prevent food sticking to them when it is cooked.

Knead Squeeze, stretch and turn a mixture, usually bread dough, before baking.

Season Add just enough salt and pepper to a recipe to suit your own tastes.

Sift/sieve Shake, tap or press an ingredient through a sieve to remove any lumps and sometimes to add air.

Simmer Cook food over a low heat on the stove top, usually after it has boiled, so that it bubbles gently.

Whisk Beat very hard and fast to add air to a mixture, usually egg whites or cream, until the mixture is light, fluffy and sometimes stiff. This can be done with a hand whisk or an electric mixer.

Things to Have in the Kitchen

Kitchen shops and supermarkets are the best places to go if you want to buy cooking equipment. Here are some of the main things you will need in the kitchen to make the recipes on the following pages.

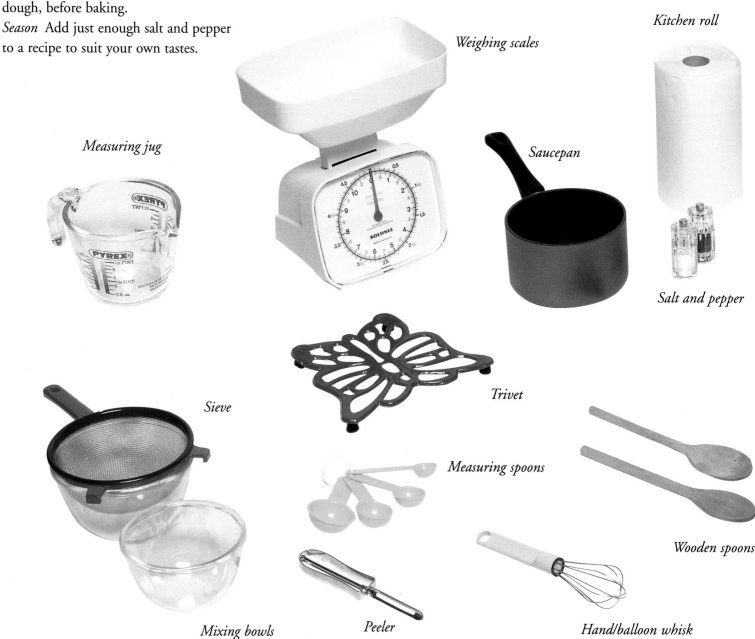

Weighing scales

Kitchen roll

Measuring jug

Saucepan

Salt and pepper

Sieve

Trivet

Measuring spoons

Mixing bowls

Peeler

Hand/balloon whisk

Wooden spoons

Knives for chopping and slicing should be sharp. Always have a grown-up nearby when using them. Other knives are useful for spreading or cutting soft things.

Wooden spoons for stirring, beating and mixing ingredients.

A rolling pin comes in handy for rolling pastry and dough.

Cutters and stamps made of metal or plastic are great fun for cutting out biscuits and sandwiches.

Mixing bowls for stirring, beating and mixing ingredients.

Saucepans and a frying pan for cooking on the stove top.

Weighing scales for weighing out ingredients.

A food processor or blender is handy for puréeing ingredients and mixing.

A grater is used for grating cheese and vegetables.

A can opener is used for taking the tops off cans.

A hand/balloon whisk is necessary for whisking air into things like eggs and cream.

A palette knife is ideal for spreading soft things, such as icing, and flipping pancakes.

A measuring jug is used for measuring liquid ingredients, such as milk and water.

A chopping board is needed for chopping and slicing things on. It is more hygienic than working directly on to the work surface or table top.

Measuring spoons are needed for measuring small amounts of ingredients, wet and dry. Most useful are 15 ml (1 tbsp) and 5 ml (1 tsp).

Sieves are used for getting the lumps out of ingredients.

Dish towels and oven gloves are for holding hot things, and putting dishes into and taking them out of the oven.

A trivet is used for putting hot pans on, as it protects the work surfaces.

A peeler is used for removing the outer layer from vegetables.

Salt and pepper are used to season (add flavour to) food.

Kitchen roll is handy for mopping up spillages, as well as absorbing excess grease from food.

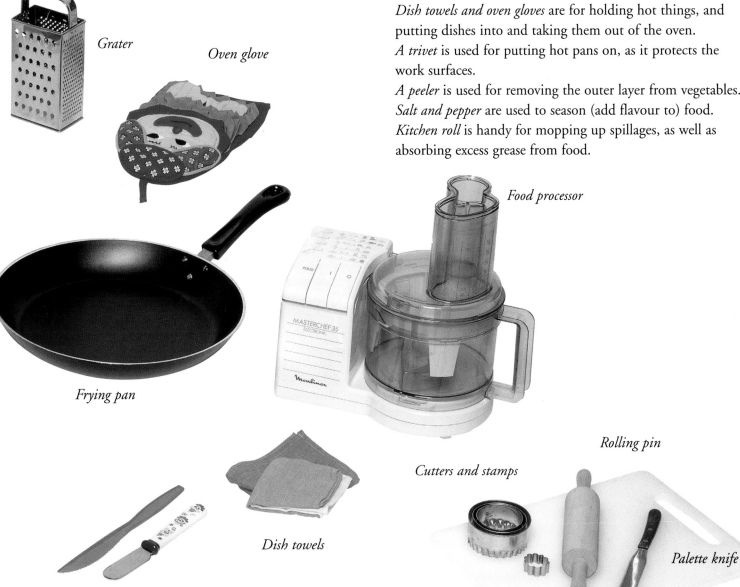

Grater

Oven glove

Food processor

Frying pan

Rolling pin

Cutters and stamps

Dish towels

Palette knife

Knives

Chopping board

Egg Bugs and Toadstools

A good thing about this recipe is that you can make the egg bugs and toadstools up to two hours in advance and keep them in the fridge. But don't dot on the mayonnaise. This should be done at the last minute, just before you serve them. Follow what Alexandra is doing and then choose who gets an egg bug and who gets a toadstool.

Handy hints:

❖ To hard boil the eggs, ask a grown-up to put them in a pan of cold water, bring to the boil and then simmer for about 10 minutes. To cool them down quickly after cooking, drain and return to the saucepan, then place them under cold running water for a few minutes.

❖ Don't bang the eggs too hard when you are trying to crack the shells to peel them. Just tap them gently on the work surface, turning them over as you tap, until the shell is cracked all over. Carefully peel away the shell, without damaging the egg white. It is easier to do this under cold running water.

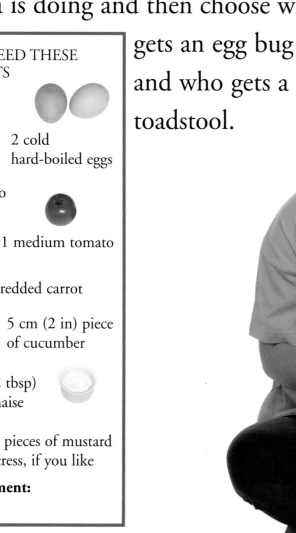

YOU WILL NEED THESE INGREDIENTS

Serves 2

2 cold hard-boiled eggs

1 cherry tomato

1 medium tomato

100 g (4 oz) shredded carrot

5 cm (2 in) piece of cucumber

30ml (2 tbsp) mayonnaise

a few pieces of mustard and cress, if you like

Special equipment:
cocktail stick

1 Peel the eggs – see handy hints opposite. Cut a thin slice from the side of one of the eggs, and a slice from the pointed end of the other egg.

2 Cut the cherry tomato in half and then cut one half into four pieces to make the egg bug. Cut the big tomato in half for the toadstool.

3 To make a base on the serving dish, arrange the shredded carrot on a plate, spreading it out so that it is flat and even.

4 Peel away strips of cucumber skin and cut two slices to stand the eggs on. You can cut more for decoration.

5 Place the cucumber slices on top of the shredded carrot, then put an egg on top of each one. Don't forget that the egg bug lies down and the toadstool stands up!

6 To finish off the egg bug, use a cocktail stick to put some mayonnaise on the big end and top of the lying-down egg. Stick on half a cherry tomato for the face and two quarters on top for the spikes. Put a blob of mayonnaise on top of the toadstool egg and put a larger tomato half on top.

7 Use the cocktail stick to put tiny spots of mayonnaise all over the toadstool and to make the eyes, nose and mouth for the egg bug's face. Use mustard and cress for the egg bug's feet.

Cheese Dip with Dunks

This dish that George is making is great for a party and all your friends will love dunking their favourite crisps and vegetables into the rich and creamy dip. Watch out for dunkin' grown-ups, they are bound to want to join in all the fun! If you want to give the strips of vegetables for dunking a crinkled effect, use a crinkle-bladed knife to cut them.

YOU WILL NEED THESE INGREDIENTS
Serves 8–10

225 g (8 oz) carton of full-fat soft cheese

60 ml (4 tbsp) milk

small bunch of fresh chives

1 small carrot, peeled

For dunking: 7.5 cm (3 in) strips of cucumber, ½ of a red, orange and yellow pepper, seeded and cut into strips, 4 baby sweetcorn, tortilla chips 8–10 cherry tomatoes
Special equipment: scissors

Handy hints:

❖ If you prefer your dips to be less rich tasting, you could use a low-fat soft cheese instead of full-fat soft cheese.
❖ Chives are a fresh herb which look a little like grass and taste of onions. If you can't find any, you can snip the green tops off spring onions instead.
❖ You could also add celery, cauliflower florets, carrot sticks, slices of apple and radishes to your selection of dipping vegetables.

1 Spoon the full-fat soft cheese into a mixing bowl and beat it with a wooden spoon until soft and creamy.

2 Add the milk to the cheese, a little at a time. Beat the mixture well each time you pour more milk in.

3 Beat the mixture hard for about 2 minutes. If necessary, add more milk to make the dip runnier.

4 Cut the chives finely and add to the cheese mixture, saving some.

5 Grate the carrot on the smallest holes of the grater. Save some and stir the rest into the cheese mixture.

6 Spoon the mixture into a bowl and sprinkle on the remaining chives and grated carrot. Cut the cucumber, baby sweetcorn and peppers for dunking into thin strips.

7 Place the bowl of dip in the centre of a serving plate and arrange little groups of the strips for dunking around the edges. Add the tomatoes and crisps or tortilla chips and let your guests start dippin' and dunkin'.

Pasta Shapes with Lentil Sauce

Tania is having great fun making this colourful and healthy dish. When you go shopping for the ingredients you need for this recipe, look out for fun pasta shapes, such as animals, vehicles or letters of the alphabet. If you can't find them, any small pasta shapes will do. This is a great recipe for your vegetarian friends because it contains no meat. Check whether the lentils need to be soaked before cooking. If so, follow the instructions on the packet.

Handy hints:

❖ Although the food processor or blender is safe to use once the lid is on properly, it is a good idea to ask a grown-up to help with the tricky stages of inserting and removing the sharp blade.

❖ Another way of serving this recipe is on a large serving platter. Put it in the centre of the table and let everyone help themselves.

YOU WILL NEED THESE INGREDIENTS

Serves 4–6

 1 garlic clove, peeled, 1 vegetable stock cube

dash of olive oil

 1 onion, peeled and chopped

175 g (6 oz) red lentils, washed and drained

 10 ml (2 tsp) tomato purée

575 ml (1 pt) water   pepper

225 g (8 oz) pasta shapes   50 g (2 oz) grated Cheddar cheese

10 ml (2 tsp) chopped, fresh parsley

Special equipment:
garlic press, food processor

1 Place the garlic clove in the garlic press and squeeze really hard to crush it.

2 Put the crushed garlic in a saucepan. Add the olive oil, chopped onion, lentils and tomato purée. Stir well.

3 Add the water to the saucepan, pouring it over the lentils and other ingredients. Stir again to mix.

4 Crumble the stock cube into the saucepan. Season with pepper, then ask a grown-up to simmer the mixture on the stove top for about 15–20 minutes, until the lentils are cooked.

5 While the lentils are cooking, weigh the pasta shapes. Put the pasta in a saucepan and ask a grown-up to cover it in boiling water, simmer for about 8–10 minutes until tender and drain. Return the pasta to the saucepan, and replace the lid.

6 Ask a grown-up to sieve the hot lentil sauce to remove some of the liquid, leaving a thick, sloppy texture. Put this in a food processor or blender. With the lid of the food processor or blender on tight, press the button to purée the lentil mixture.

7 Ask the grown-up to remove the sharp blade from the food processor or blender. Serve the pasta on to plates and spoon the lentil sauce on top.

Garnish the finished dish with a sprinkling of grated cheese and a little chopped, fresh parsley. Delicious!

Funny Face Pizzas

Use your imagination to make your pizzas look happy or sad or just plain silly. Choose your ingredients to suit the expression you want. You can also make up your own hair styles for the pizza faces as Karina has done here, using as much or as little of the mustard and cress as you like. If you don't want a bow tie, then put the kiwi fruit in the hair as a ribbon.

Handy hints:
❖ If you prefer your pizzas slightly flatter, use small round pitta breads instead of burger buns.
❖ If you don't like or can't get mozzarella cheese, use Cheddar cheese instead. It is just as delicious but won't be so 'stringy' when you eat it.

YOU WILL NEED THESE INGREDIENTS
Serves 2

1 large burger bun, split into two halves

30 ml (2 tbsp) tomato and onion pizza topping from a jar

75 g (3 oz) piece mozzarella cheese

1 mushroom

¼ green pepper, seeded and cut into thin slices

1 carton of mustard and crees

4 round slices of peeled kiwi fruit and a grape

Special equipment: rolling pin, small flower-shaped biscuit cutter

1 Put the bun halves on the work surface. Flatten them gently and evenly all over using the rolling pin.

2 Spread tomato and onion pizza topping over the top of each bun, making sure it goes close to the edges.

3 Cut the piece of mozzarella cheese into thin slices. You could ask a grown-up to do this with a sharp knife.

4 Using the flower-shaped cutter, stamp out four pieces of cheese for the pizzas' eyes. Put two in position on each of the pizza bases and set aside.

5 Wash the mushroom and slice it in half to make two noses. Position the noses on the pizza faces and press down lightly.

6 Use the green pepper slices to make mouths on the faces. Put the pizzas on the grill pan and ask a grown-up to cook them under a hot grill for about 5 minutes, until the cheese has melted a little and the buns are toasted around the edges.

7 Ask the grown-up to put the pizzas on to serving plates. Cut bunches of the cress with scissors or a knife and put them in neat piles around the top of the faces to look like hair.

Cut the kiwi rounds and grape in half and position them on the plates to make ears and bow ties.

Swimming Fish Cakes

There are lots of variations on this recipe that Joshua is making. You could serve the swimming fish on a sea of your favourite vegetable. Try a sea of peas or sweetcorn, or a mixture of both. If you particularly like modelling, make lots of tiny fish, and serve everyone with two or more. But remember to tell your grown-up helper that the small fish won't take as long to cook as the bigger ones.

Handy hints:
❖ Ask a grown-up to open the can of tuna with a can opener, as this can be dangerous and you might cut yourself.
❖ You could make the fish cake mixture and even shape the cakes up to several hours in advance, if you like. Keep them in the fridge until you are ready to cook and eat them.

YOU WILL NEED THESE INGREDIENTS
Serves 4

3 large potatoes

25 g (1 oz) butter

1 egg   dash of milk

200 g (7 oz) can tuna chunks in brine, drained

75 g (3 oz) fresh breadcrumbs

pepper

oil, for shallow frying

For the garnish:
4 peas

a few sprigs of fresh curly parsley

½ cucumber peeled, cut in half lengthways and very thinly sliced, 4 slices of lemon, 4 thin slices of tomato

Special equipment: vegetable peeler, potato masher, can opener

1 Peel the potatoes with the peeler, cut into small pieces and put in the saucepan. Cover with water. Ask a grown-up to boil the potatoes for about 15–20 minutes, until soft.

2 Ask a grown-up to drain the potatoes and return them to the saucepan. Place the saucepan on a trivet. Add the butter, milk and egg.

3 Put a dish towel between you and the saucepan to prevent you touching the hot saucepan. Mash the potatoes using the masher until they are smooth, with no lumps.

4 Spoon the mashed potato into a mixing bowl, making sure you scrape it all out of the saucepan. Use a wooden spoon to mix in the tuna, breadcrumbs and pepper. Place the bowl of potato mixture in the fridge to chill for about 30 minutes.

5 Take the bowl out of the fridge and wet your hands slightly. Divide the mixture into four equal portions and, working on a chopping board, mould them into fish shapes.

6 Ask a grown-up to shallow fry the fish cakes in hot oil for about 5 minutes on both sides. Drain the fish cakes on absorbent kitchen paper and transfer to the serving plate.

To garnish your swimming fish, put a pea in position for the eye and a slice of tomato for the mouth of each fish. Use fresh parsley for air bubbles and a lemon slice for the sun in the sky. Arrange the cucumber slices in rows to look like the sea.

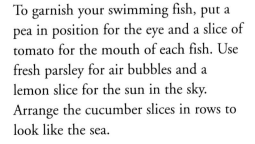

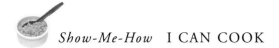

Ham and Sweetcorn Roll-ups

With George's delicious recipe any day can be pancake day, so get flipping and tossing. Those with a big appetite can probably eat two roll-ups, otherwise serve one per person. If you and your grown-up helper manage to make them really thin, you might be able to make a few extra to serve sprinkled with sugar and lemon juice or with jam, for a totally pancake meal.

Handy hints:
❖ The frying pan should be very hot before cooking the pancakes, so ask a grown-up to help you.
❖ When you put the rolled pancakes on the baking sheet to heat through in the oven, make sure you space them a little apart. If you don't, they might stick together and break up when you transfer them to the serving plates.
❖ You can, if you prefer, sprinkle the pancakes with cheese and ask a grown-up to melt the cheese under the grill.

YOU WILL NEED THESE INGREDIENTS
Serves 3–6

100 g (4 oz) plain flour

small pinch of salt

1 egg

150 ml (¼ pt) milk

olive oil, for greasing

For the filling: 2 thick slices of lean (not fatty) ham

25 g (1 oz) frozen chopped spinach, thawed

50 g (2 oz) full-fat soft cheese

25 g (1 oz) canned sweetcorn, drained

pepper

100 g (4 oz) grated Cheddar cheese

Special equipment: can opener, ballon whisk, palette knife, baking sheet

1 Preheat the oven to 200°C/400°F/ Gas 6. Put the flour, salt, milk and egg into a mixing jug. Whisk together until runny and smooth.

2 Ask a grown-up to coat the bottom of a hot, oiled frying pan with the batter. Cook for 1 minute each side and flip with a palette knife.

3 Ask the grown-up to continue making the pancakes. Meanwhile cut the ham into strips and then into squares and put in a mixing bowl.

4 Add the spinach, full-fat soft cheese and sweetcorn to the mixing bowl with the ham. Season the filling mixture with a little pepper, if you like.

5 Stir the filling mixture well, until all the ingredients are mixed in. Lay the pancakes on the work surface.

6 Spoon some of the filling mixture on to each pancake, placing it along the edge nearest you. Roll the pancake around the filling and keep rolling until the filling is completely wrapped up in the pancake.

Finally, place the filled pancakes on a baking sheet and ask a grown-up to bake them for about 15 minutes, until warmed through. Transfer the pancakes on to serving plates and sprinkle with grated cheese to garnish.

Colourful Chicken Kebabs

You'll have a great time making your own kebabs and choosing what you put on them. They're brilliant to cook under the grill as Tania is doing here, or on the barbecue with the help of a grown-up. It is best to wash and prepare all the vegetables before you begin threading them on to the skewers. This will help you decide the order of ingredients and stop you getting in a muddle.

Handy hints:
❖ To make your own delicious salad dressing, mix 60 ml (4 tbsp) sunflower oil, 30 ml (2 tbsp) vinegar, 15 ml (1 tbsp) clear honey, and a dash of pepper together in a jar with a tight-fitting lid, then shake it well.
❖ Your grown-up helper may need to add a little more boiling water to the rice while it is cooking, if it looks as if it is drying out before it is cooked.
❖ The reason for soaking the skewers is to prevent them burning during grilling. If they have been soaked in water first, they will not burn so easily.

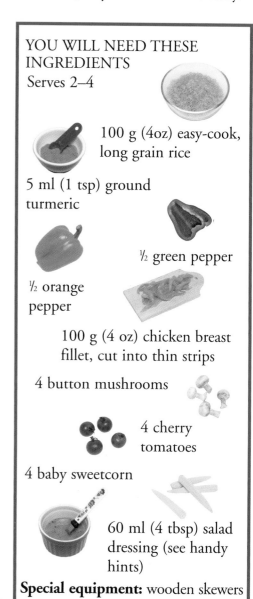

YOU WILL NEED THESE INGREDIENTS
Serves 2–4

100 g (4oz) easy-cook, long grain rice

5 ml (1 tsp) ground turmeric

½ green pepper

½ orange pepper

100 g (4 oz) chicken breast fillet, cut into thin strips

4 button mushrooms

4 cherry tomatoes

4 baby sweetcorn

60 ml (4 tbsp) salad dressing (see handy hints)

Special equipment: wooden skewers

1 Put the wooden skewers in a shallow dish of cold water. Leave them to soak in the water for about 30 minutes, then remove them and throw away the water.

2 Put the rice and turmeric in a saucepan. Ask a grown-up to cover it with boiling water, simmer for 15 minutes, then drain. Return the rice to the saucepan and cover with a lid.

3 While the rice is cooking, put the peppers on a chopping board and cut out the white seeds and pith inside. Rinse the peppers under cold water and cut them into chunks.

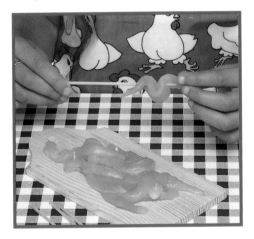

4 Thread the chicken on to the skewers as shown. This will give a coiled effect when it cooks.

5 Thread the other ingredients on to the skewers in whatever order you like. Make sure you finish each one with a piece of baby sweetcorn, pushing the skewer only a little way in.

6 Put the kebabs on the grill pan and drizzle over some of the salad dressing. Ask a grown-up to put the kebabs under a hot grill for about 5 minutes, then to turn them over and continue grilling for another 5 minutes, until the chicken is cooked.

7 Just before the kebabs are cooked, put some rice on to the serving plates and spread it out.

Arrange the kebabs on the rice and they are ready to serve.

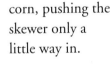
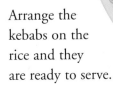

Crazy Popcorn

This multi-coloured cheesy mixture that Andreas is making will make your party the talk of the town. Have fun choosing your own colours for the popcorn and cheese. If you can't get or don't like Red Leicester or Sage Derby, use yellow Cheddar cheese instead. And if you haven't got a large enough container to hold all of the popcorn, or have a lot of guests who are going to want to eat at once, then fill two containers instead.

Handy hints:
❖ You must use powdered food colouring as liquid colouring will turn the popcorn soggy. You will find the powdered kind in specialist cake decorating shops.
❖ You can buy microwave popcorn which is especially for cooking in the microwave. Follow the instructions on the packet for cooking (ask a grown-up to operate the microwave) and colour it as directed in steps 4–6.

YOU WILL NEED THESE
INGREDIENTS
  Serves 10–15

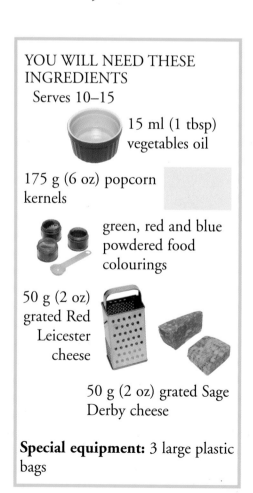

15 ml (1 tbsp) vegetables oil

175 g (6 oz) popcorn kernels

green, red and blue powdered food colourings

50 g (2 oz) grated Red Leicester cheese

50 g (2 oz) grated Sage Derby cheese

Special equipment: 3 large plastic bags

1 Put the vegetable oil in a large saucepan. Pour in the popcorn kernels and stir with a wooden spoon to coat them all in the oil.

2 Place the lid on the saucepan and ask a grown-up to heat the popcorn on the stove top, gently, for about 5 minutes, until you hear the popcorn starting to pop. Do not remove the lid.

3 When the popping noises have slowed down and you hardly hear any popping at all, ask the grown-up to put the saucepan on a trivet on the table. You can now remove the lid.

4 Put small amounts of popcorn in each plastic bag. The bags should be see-through so you can see the colour of the popcorn changing when you add the colour.

5 Use a tiny spoon to add a small amount of food colouring to each of the bags of popcorn. You can choose what colours you use and how much popcorn you want to make a particular colour.

6 Close the bag and hold it tightly in one hand. Shake the bag and tap it with the other hand, tossing the popcorn inside the bag to coat it evenly in the colouring. As you colour each batch, tip it into a large bowl.

7 When all the popcorn is coloured, add the grated cheese.

Wash your hands, then carefully toss the mixture together evenly. Try not to tip it over the sides of the container.

Frozen Banana Lollies

These lollies are great for a summer party. But if you haven't got any party plans, just make a batch of lollies and freeze them all for yourself. They will keep in the freezer, in sealed bags, for about a month. Sophie has coated her lollies with coconut, but if you don't like it, choose your own coating. Try toasted, chopped nuts or crumbled chocolate flake bars. They are all delicious!

Handy hints:
❖ You can buy lolly sticks in most hardware shops and supermarkets, but if you want to be crafty and environmentally friendly collect up your own and your friends' used ones. Wash and dry them and they'll be as good as new!
❖ Don't peel the bananas too early, otherwise they will start to go brown and mushy.

YOU WILL NEED THESE INGREDIENTS
Serves 8

100 g (4 oz) desiccated coconut

red, blue and green food colourings (powdered or liquid)

8 small bananas

a little maple syrup

Special equipment: 8 lolly sticks, pastry brush, baking sheet, clear film

68

1 Divide the coconut into three small bowls and add a small amount of food colouring to each. Stir well, until the coconut is evenly coloured.

2 Pour the red, blue and green coloured coconut on to separate plates and spread it out evenly.

3 Peel the bananas and cut a small piece off one end of each one, to make it straight. Carefully press a lolly stick into the straight end of each banana, taking care not to push the stick in too far, as it might break through the side.

4 Pour some maple syrup into a bowl. Holding the lolly stick and using a pastry brush, brush an even coating of maple syrup over each banana. Put on a plate when coated.

5 Still holding the lolly sticks, dip and roll the bananas in the coloured coconut until they are coated evenly.

6 Lay the bananas on a baking sheet covered with clear film. The bananas must not touch. Freeze for 4 hours.

Take the banana lollies off the baking sheet and arrange on a serving plate. Ideally you should wait about 15 minutes, to let the bananas soften a little before you eat them.

Cut-out Cookies

Any cutter, any shape and any size is good for this recipe. You can also use chocolate sugar strands or flaked chocolate, or even chopped, coloured glacé cherries as decoration. Whatever you choose, be sure to make lots as Alex is doing, because these yummy biscuits will certainly get eaten up very quickly. It's a good idea to have a second baking sheet and a second serving plate handy!

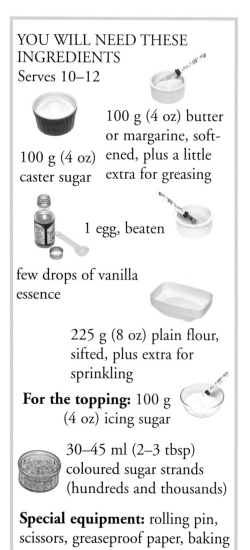

YOU WILL NEED THESE
INGREDIENTS
Serves 10–12

100 g (4 oz) caster sugar

100 g (4 oz) butter or margarine, softened, plus a little extra for greasing

1 egg, beaten

few drops of vanilla essence

225 g (8 oz) plain flour, sifted, plus extra for sprinkling

For the topping: 100 g (4 oz) icing sugar

30–45 ml (2–3 tbsp) coloured sugar strands (hundreds and thousands)

Special equipment: rolling pin, scissors, greaseproof paper, baking tray, biscuit cutters in different shapes, wire cooling rack

Handy hints:
❖ To save your energy, ask a grown-up to help you use an electric hand mixer to make the dough, or you could make it in a food processor.
❖ When you have cut out the first lot of biscuits from the rolled out dough, gather up all the trimmings and roll them out again. Now you can cut out another lot of biscuits. Keep doing this until all the biscuit dough is used up.
❖ Before you start to drizzle the icing over the biscuits, put a big sheet of greaseproof paper under the wire rack. This will catch all the drips of icing and when you are finished, you just gather up the paper and throw it away.

1 Preheat the oven to 200°C/400°F/ Gas 6. Put the butter and sugar in a mixing bowl and beat with a wooden spoon, until light and fluffy.

2 Add the egg and a few drops of vanilla essence and keep beating until the mixture is smooth.

3 Carefully stir in the flour, mixing well, until a stiff dough starts to form in the bowl.

4 Flour the board and your hands and knead the dough until smooth. Sprinkle more flour and roll out the dough until quite thin. Keep your rolling pin well floured to stop it sticking to the dough.

5 Put a greased sheet of greaseproof paper on to a greased baking tray. Using the cutters, cut out the biscuit shapes and place them on the baking tray. Ask a grown-up to bake the biscuits for 10 minutes.

6 Ask a grown-up to put the biscuits on a wire rack to cool. Put the icing sugar in a bowl and stir in about 15 ml (1 tbsp) of cold water. Mix well.

7 Use a teaspoon to drizzle the icing over the biscuits.

Sprinkle the coloured sugar strands over the biscuits, to decorate. Put the finished biscuits on a plate. Do not pile them up or they will stick. Leave the biscuits for about 30 minutes to let the icing set, then serve.

Cake-cream Cones

Handy hints:
❖ Make sure you don't press the cakes too firmly into the cones, otherwise the cones might break.
❖ Use separate knives for the different icing colours, otherwise you'll mix the colours and they will look messy.
❖ The cake-cream cones can be made up to 3 hours in advance and kept in the fridge.

These cones that Alex, Sophie and Otis are eating will fool everybody. If you put them on the table with lots of decorations around them, all your guests will think they're real ice-cream.

YOU WILL NEED THESE INGREDIENTS
Serves 3

100 g (4 oz) fondant moulding icing

175 g (6 oz) icing sugar

75 g (3 oz) butter or margarine, softened

30–45 ml (2–3 tbsp) milk

green and pink food colourings, 10 ml (2 tsp) cocoa

3 small fairy cakes

coloured sugar strands, chocolate sugar strands

3 ice-cream cones

chocolate flake bars and wafers, to decorate

Special equipment: egg boxes (one large or two small), foil, pencil

1 To make holders for the cones, turn the egg boxes upside-down. Press the fondant icing into the hollows, shaping a hole to support the bottom of the cones.

2 Cover the boxes in foil, making sure the joins are underneath. Place on the work surface, with the filled hollows on top. Feel the hollows, then pierce the foil with a pencil.

3 To make butter icing, put the icing sugar in a mixing bowl with the butter or margarine and the milk. Use a wooden spoon to mix the icing until it is smooth and creamy.

4 Divide the butter icing into three bowls. Add a speck of food colouring to two bowls and the cocoa to the third. Mix until evenly coloured.

5 Remove any paper from the bottom of the fairy cakes. Gently press a cake into the top of a cone, twisting it slightly until it stays in. Repeat with the other cakes and cones.

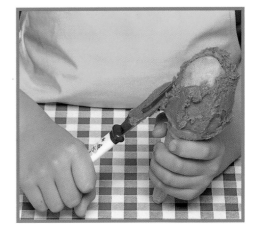

6 Spread the icing on to the cake, working from the top downwards. Put the cone in the stand to hold it safely while you coat the rest.

7 Sprinkle with sugar strands, and lightly press chocolate flake bars and wafers into the cakes.

Jelly Pond

By moulding fondant icing just like play-dough, you can be really creative with this recipe and make your own monsters for a lake or pond scene. Follow what Sophie is doing to see how. Try water snakes, ducks, waterlilies, fish and frogs. Your lake or pond will be even more realistic if you add a spot of green food colouring to the jelly while you are dissolving it.

Handy hints:
❖ It is a good idea to wear rubber gloves when you are colouring the fondant icing, otherwise your hands will get coloured too.
❖ The easiest way to get the colour of the icing even is to roll it out into a sausage shape, bring the two ends of the sausage together and start rolling out a new sausage. Carry on in this way until you are happy with the colour.
❖ Put the chopped jelly into the 'creature' bowl at the very last minute before serving, as the 'wet' jelly will make the fondant creatures start to leak some of their colour.

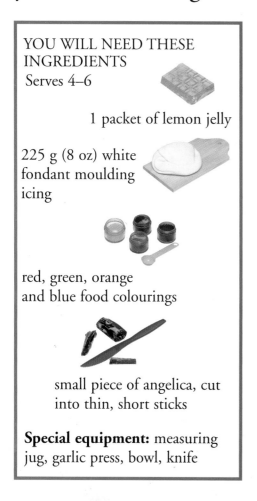

YOU WILL NEED THESE INGREDIENTS
Serves 4–6

1 packet of lemon jelly

225 g (8 oz) white fondant moulding icing

red, green, orange and blue food colourings

small piece of angelica, cut into thin, short sticks

Special equipment: measuring jug, garlic press, bowl, knife

1 Break the jelly into small pieces and put it in the mixing jug.

2 With a grown-up, make the jelly according to the packet instructions. Put in the fridge to set.

3 Divide the fondant icing into four portions. Add a speck of food colouring to each, then roll and knead it in.

4 Shape your pond creatures and waterlilies, and press the angelica sticks into a blob of icing for the reeds. Put the shapes for the surface on a plate to dry.

5 To decorate the inside of the jelly bowl, press your underwater creatures to the glass on the inside. Brush a little water on to the creatures' fronts to help them stick better.

6 To make the pond grass, take a small piece of green fondant icing and put it inside a garlic press. Squeeze hard with two hands and watch the grass come out. Use a knife to cut off the grass and put it on a plate to dry and harden.

7 When the jelly is set, use a knife to stir and chop the jelly into tiny pieces. Spoon the jelly into the bowl, taking care not to knock the creatures.

Position all the shapes for the surface of the pond. Make a little scene with the ducks swimming in the pond with the waterlilies and grass all around. Serve immediately.

I Can Paint

Star and Moon Stencilled Gift Wrap

If you have always wanted to make your own special gift wrap and matching greetings cards, now is your chance.

The moon and star shapes that Kirsty is stencilling are simple. She is only using gold paint, but you can use lots of different colours. If you want to stencil with lots of colours, use a different sponge for each colour and let each colour dry thoroughly before you add the next.

Stencilling technique

Stencilling is great fun and easy to do. For the best results, the paint needs to be thick, so don't mix any water with it. Do not use too much paint on the sponge, and apply it with a light dabbing movement. You can always go over it again to add more colour.

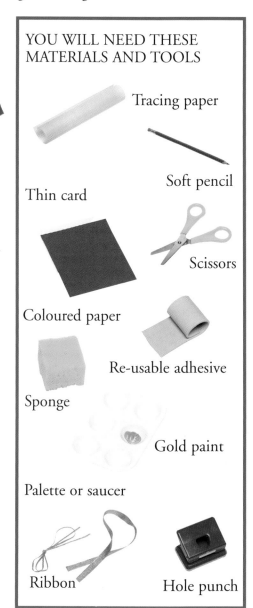

YOU WILL NEED THESE MATERIALS AND TOOLS

Tracing paper

Soft pencil

Thin card

Scissors

Coloured paper

Re-usable adhesive

Sponge

Gold paint

Palette or saucer

Ribbon

Hole punch

1 Using a soft pencil, trace the star and moon templates from the front of the book on to card.

2 Use the scissors to make a hole in the middle of the design, and then cut towards the shape. You should have three different stencils.

3 Place the stencils on the coloured paper. Secure them with re-usable adhesive. Dab the sponge in the gold paint and sponge over the stencils.

4 Let the paint dry, then move the stencils to another space on the paper and repeat. Continue until you have covered the whole sheet with gold moons and stars.

5 When the paint is completely dry, use the sheet of paper to wrap up a present. To make the gift extremely luxurious, add a gold ribbon and tie a bow.

6 Cut out a small piece of paper and stencil it in the same way to make a gift tag for the present. Using a hole puncher, make a hole in the corner and slip a piece of gold ribbon through.

7 Here a moon is being stencilled on to a card for a different design.

A unique set of gift wrap for a very special present.

Christmas Crackers

Your family and friends will be delighted when you present them with these pretty crackers at the Christmas meal or at a party. You must plan this project in advance as you need a cardboard tube for each cracker.

Jessica is using traditional Christmas shapes and colours in her design, but you could choose your own instead.

Presents galore

If you are feeling generous you could also put a little gift inside each cracker, and perhaps write a joke to go inside as well. This should be done in step 7, when you have closed only one end of the cracker.

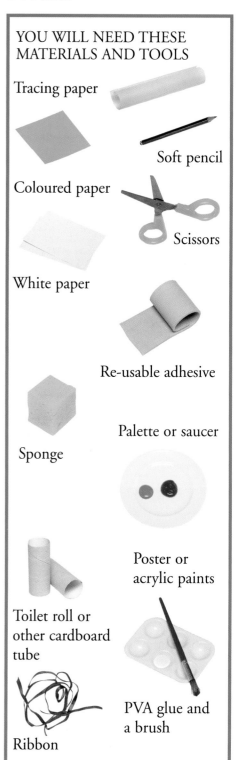

YOU WILL NEED THESE MATERIALS AND TOOLS

Tracing paper

Soft pencil

Coloured paper

Scissors

White paper

Re-usable adhesive

Sponge

Palette or saucer

Toilet roll or other cardboard tube

Poster or acrylic paints

Ribbon

PVA glue and a brush

1 Trace the holly leaf and Christmas tree templates from the front of the book on to coloured paper and cut them out.

2 Scatter the shapes over the white paper, sticking them down with a piece of re-usable adhesive. Your pattern can be regular or random.

3 Dab the sponge into one of the paints. Wipe off any excess on the side of the palette. Sponge over all the shapes on the paper.

4 Rinse the sponge out under the tap, squeezing it as dry as you can. Dab it in the second paint colour and sponge over the shapes again.

5 When the sheet of paper is completely dry, gently peel the templates away to reveal a colourful Christmas design. Place it face down on your work surface.

6 Brush glue all over the cardboard tube. Place it halfway along one edge of the sheet of paper. Carefully roll the paper around the tube. Glue the edge down.

7 Feel where the ends of the tube are and pinch in the paper there. Finally, cut triangles from the ends of the paper and add ribbons.

The ideal table decoration for a Christmas party.

Painted Stones Caterpillar

If you are unable to get to the seaside to collect the pebbles, make some from self-hardening clay which can be bought in craft and hobby shops. When you have painted the pebbles with pictures or numbers, you will have hours of fun with them. Joshua is being clever with his pebbles by painting a caterpillar on one side and numbers and mathematical signs on the other, so that he can practise his sums and see how brainy he is.

Painting tips

You will find it easier to paint half of all the stones, then go back and finish them off. In this way, you won't be trying to hold an area of stone that is already wet.

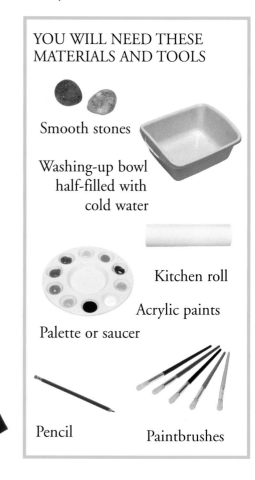

YOU WILL NEED THESE MATERIALS AND TOOLS

Smooth stones

Washing-up bowl half-filled with cold water

Kitchen roll

Acrylic paints

Palette or saucer

Pencil

Paintbrushes

1 Wash the stones in the washing-up bowl and dry them well with kitchen roll. Use as many as you like.

2 Paint the stones. Try to make each one a different colour. Leave them on your work surface until they are completely dry.

3 Arrange the stones in a long line with the biggest at one end and the smallest at the other. Draw a caterpillar design on them.

4 Paint the caterpillar's body using different colours. Use black, brown or another dark colour for its feet.

5 Decorate each part of its body with different coloured spots. You can vary the size of the spots too.

6 Either use a new set of painted stones, or wait until the caterpillar is dry and turn the stones over. Paint in some figures and mathematical symbols.

None of your papers will blow away when the caterpillar is weighing them down.

7 Impress your family and friends by showing them how clever you are.

Butterfly Blottography Box

Blottography prints are easy to do and the results are always an exciting surprise. This technique is at least 100 years old. Alice is using her prints to brighten up a storage box, but you could also stick a blottography shape to a tray and varnish over it – ask a grown-up to help with this.

Blottography technique
Be sure to use a large piece of paper for your prints so that paint doesn't ooze out over everything and make a mess.

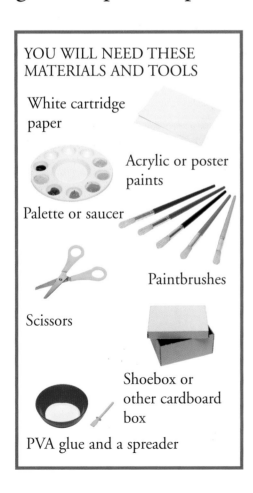

YOU WILL NEED THESE MATERIALS AND TOOLS

White cartridge paper

Acrylic or poster paints

Palette or saucer

Paintbrushes

Scissors

Shoebox or other cardboard box

PVA glue and a spreader

1 Make sure that your sheet of paper is longer than it is wide. Fold it in half lengthways.

2 Open up the paper and dab generous spots of paint on one side only. Use as many different colours as you like, but don't get it *too* runny.

3 Fold the paper in half once again, bringing the dry side over on to the wet side. Carefully smooth it down with your hand.

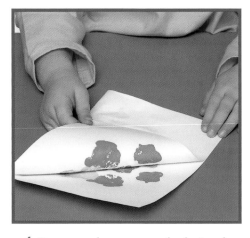

4 Open up the paper and admire the colourful, symmetrical pattern you have created on both sides of the paper. Leave it to dry thoroughly.

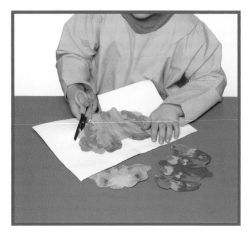

5 Make some more patterns of different sizes and using different colour combinations in the same way. Try using all pale colours or all dark. Cut them out when they are dry.

A colourful way of storing your odds and ends.

6 Paint the cardboard box inside and out. If you are using a shoe-box, or any other box that was coloured to start with, you will find it easier to cover the existing colour if you use acrylic paint. Poster paint is fine if your box is white to start with.

7 When the box is completely dry, glue your patterns to the box.

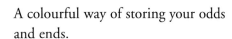

Vegetable-print T-shirts

Sasha is using different colours and all sorts of vegetables on a white T-shirt. If you don't want to make an all-over design, you could print just in the centre of the shirt. For a more intricate design, use smaller vegetables such as tiny onions cut in half, or a baby carrot. Use different sizes of mushroom too.

Design rules

If you are not sure about a design, print it on paper first to get a good idea of how it will look when it is on the T-shirt. Once it is on the T-shirt it will be difficult to remove or change.

YOU WILL NEED THESE MATERIALS AND TOOLS

Selection of vegetables

Chopping board

Kitchen knife

Plain T-shirt – white for preference

Newspaper

Fabric paints

Paintbrushes

1 Choose vegetables that will make interesting prints of different sizes, such as a stick of celery (semi-circle), carrot (circle), pepper (crinkly circle), mushroom and leek.

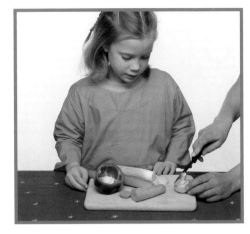

2 Ask a grown-up to cut up the vegetables for you. Make sure that they cut round the pepper – you don't want a strip – and leave the stalk on the mushroom slice.

3 Lay the T-shirt flat and front side up on your work surface. Put some newspapers inside so that your design does not go through to the back of the T-shirt.

4 Paint the edge of the pepper with fabric paint. Make sure that the edge is covered with paint but don't get it too wet or it might smudge.

5 Print the pepper on to the T-shirt. Try to hold it still while it is in contact with the shirt so that the edges don't blur. You may need to repaint it between prints.

6 Paint the end of the carrot with fabric paint and use it to print in the centre of and all around the pepper prints. Try not to print over another print as the colours may run.

7 Use all the other vegetables in the same way, choosing different colours and building up an interesting design. Leave the T-shirt to dry.

Everyone will want to know where you got your designer T-shirt.

Bubble-printed Notebook

Food colouring
If you can't find coloured inks you could use food colourings instead. You may find there are not as many different colours and most of them will be paler than some inks but you will still get good results.

It is a good idea to do bubble printing as close to the kitchen sink as you can since you need lots of water and washing-up liquid to make fluffy bubbles. Don't lift a full bowl of water yourself – ask a grown-up to do it.

The secret of bubble printing is not to pour in too many colours at once. Remember you can always add more if you don't like the first sheet.

YOU WILL NEED THESE MATERIALS AND TOOLS

Washing-up bowl

Washing-up liquid

Coloured inks

White cartridge paper

Scissors

Newspaper

Notebook

PVA glue and a spreader

92

1 Squeeze a generous amount of washing-up liquid into the washing-up bowl.

2 Add cold water and swish it around so that there are plenty of bubbles in the bowl.

3 Gradually dribble different coloured inks on to the surface of the bubbles.

4 Cut a piece of cartridge paper about the same size as the bowl. Gently lay the paper on the surface of the coloured bubbles.

5 Carefully remove the paper from the bowl and place it face up on sheets of newspaper to dry.

6 If the paper dries crinkly, flatten it by placing it in between some heavy books and leaving it overnight.

Decorate your notebooks, diary and address book with your individual bubble-printed papers.

7 Open the notebook and cut the paper, adding an extra 2.5 cm (1 in) all around. Cut across the corners and cut a V at the top and bottom of the spine. Glue the extra inside the cover.

Finger-painted Flowers

These wild and colourful flowers brighten up any room and don't even need to be watered. The great thing about making your own flowers is that you can choose which colours you want them to be and if you paint the backs and fronts differently, you can turn them round when you get bored.

Flower arranging

To make a beautiful flower arrangement put a piece of florist's foam or crumpled newspaper in the bottom of the vase. This will help to keep the flowers upright.

YOU WILL NEED THESE MATERIALS AND TOOLS

Tracing paper

Soft pencil

Thick coloured papers

Scissors

Palette or saucer

Acrylic or poster paints

PVA glue and a brush

Thin paintbrush

Sticky tape

Garden sticks

1 Using a soft pencil, trace the flower, circle and leaf templates from the front of the book on to coloured paper.

2 Using the scissors, cut out the shapes. You will need two matching flower shapes, two circles and two leaf shapes for each flower.

3 Glue a circle of coloured paper on to the centre of each flower. Make sure that the flowers and circles are different colours.

4 Dip your fingers one at a time into the paint and then press them on to your flowers. Use a different finger for each colour. Cover the flowers with finger prints.

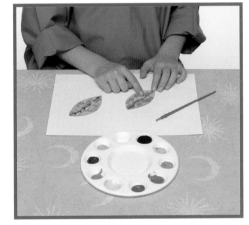

5 Leave the flowers to dry thoroughly while you make the leaves. Finger paint the leaf shapes with different green paints and paint a fine line of colour down the centre of each one to make the vein. Leave them to dry.

6 Use a piece of sticky tape to attach a garden stick to the back of a flower. Glue a matching flower on to the back and gently press it down to make sure that it sticks.

7 Attach the back of one leaf to the garden stick with sticky tape and glue a matching leaf to the back of it.

Everlasting flowers brighten up the dullest day.

Wooden-spoon Puppets

Tania and Joshua are having fun painting their puppets. Create your own theatre characters on wooden spoons then put on a show to impress the grown-ups. Hide behind the sofa and use its back as the stage. Try to give all the characters different voices too.

Drying tip

Stand the spoons in a jam jar while the wet heads dry. To dry the handles, stand the heads in a big lump of modelling clay.

YOU WILL NEED THESE MATERIALS AND TOOLS

Wooden spoons

Palette or saucer

Acrylic or poster paints

Paintbrushes

Scissors

Embroidery thread or wool

PVA glue and a brush   Ribbon

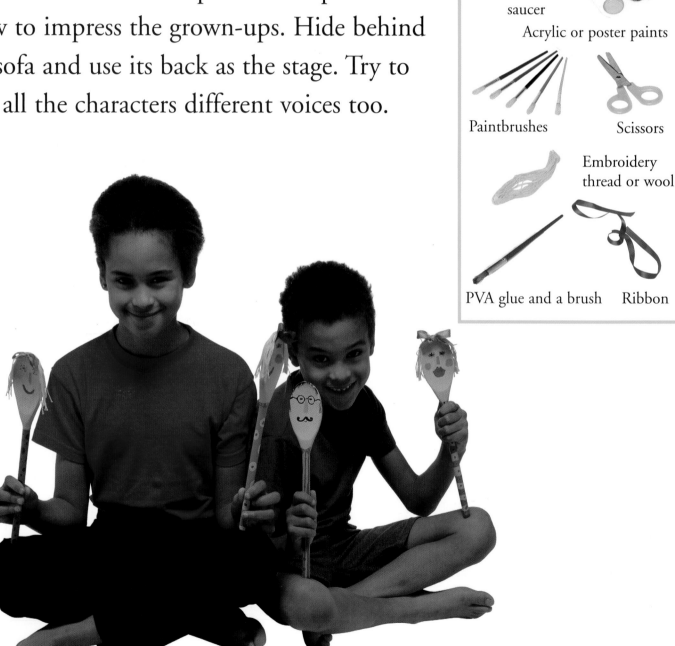

1 Paint the head of the spoon and leave it to dry.

2 Paint the handle of the spoon using a different colour and leave it to dry.

3 Decorate the handle with spots, stripes, collar, buttons or a bow tie.

4 Paint a face on to the head of the spoon and leave to dry. If you are making a man puppet, paint on some hair or, if you prefer, leave him bald.

5 If you are making a lady, cut about 15 strands of embroidery thread all the same length. Tie a shorter piece around the middle of them to keep them together.

6 Glue the hair on to the top of the lady's head and leave it to dry. Try not to use too much glue. If you do, let it dry, then peel off the excess with your fingers.

Make your own theatre and impress your friends with your own plays.

7 Tie the ribbon into a bow and glue it on to the hair.

Wax-resist Badges

Add a personal touch to a favourite outfit with a badge made with the magical technique of wax resist. Alice is using wax crayons, which give a colourful result, but the technique also works in black and white if you use a candle to draw your design. Remember that as your badge is made out of card, you can't wear it outside in the rain.

Age badges

A variation on this idea is to make an age badge for you or a friend, or your little brother or sister. Vary the colours to suit the personality of the wearer.

YOU WILL NEED THESE MATERIALS AND TOOLS

Wax crayons

White card

Paintbrush

Dark coloured poster paint

Sticky tape

Scissors

Safety pins

1 Collect together all the materials you will need for the project before you begin.

2 Draw a flowerpot shape on to the card with wax crayons. The brighter the colours, the more attractive the finished badge will be.

3 Add a cactus in a different colour, then decorate the pot and cactus using as many colours as you like.

4 Paint over your wax drawing with poster paint. Don't worry about the edges too much as you are going to cut out the picture later.

5 When the paint is completely dry, you should still be able to see your wax drawing. Cut around the edge of the cactus and flowerpot.

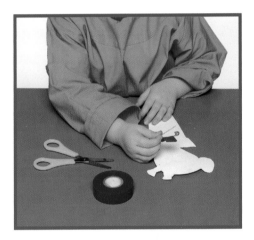

6 Turn the badge over. Cut a small piece of sticky tape and use it to attach the safety pin to the middle of the badge.

It's obvious who is on your team with these colourful badges.

Flowery Glass

These jolly flowers will liven up any glass frame. You could also use lots of smaller flower stickers to decorate a jam jar to use as a pencil pot or flower vase.

Aaron is decorating a frame but you can stick the flowers on the inside of a real window as in step 7.

Handy hints
Plastic film is quite difficult to smooth down without getting air bubbles trapped. The trick is to work slowly, peeling off a bit of backing and smoothing as you go.

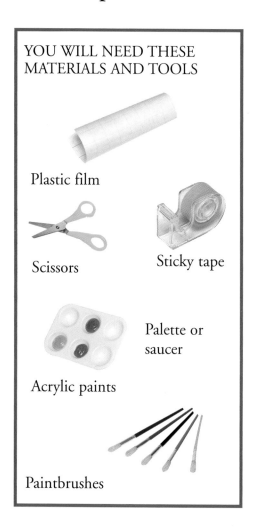

YOU WILL NEED THESE
MATERIALS AND TOOLS

Plastic film

Scissors

Sticky tape

Palette or
saucer

Acrylic paints

Paintbrushes

1 Cut two pieces of plastic film the same size. Stick the corners of one piece to your work surface with sticky tape. Do not remove the backing.

2 Paint the centre of a flower on to the centre of one piece of the film. Use a bright colour such as red, purple or yellow.

3 Using a different colour, paint five petals around the centre of the flower. Take care not to smudge the centre as you paint.

4 Decorate the flower with spots of a different, bright colour. Leave the flower to dry completely.

5 Take the second piece of film and carefully peel away the film's backing. Stick it over the flower. Work slowly, smoothing out any air bubbles with your fingers as you go.

6 If you get an air bubble, prick it with the point of a needle and smooth it out, then carefully cut around the flower.

7 Peel off the backing and stick the flower to the inside of your window.

Have year-round flowers on your bedroom window.

Flick-painted Starscape

This is a messy project so be sure to cover your work surface with lots of newspaper or scrap paper, or, if the weather is fine, do your flick painting outside. You can use any size of box for the planet story. The planet and rocket will move if you blow them or put the box by an open window.

If you want to make the inside of the box sparkle, add some glitter or cut out star shapes from kitchen foil and scatter them around the box.

Large-scale scene

A shoebox was used for this project but if you want to make a really big scene, get a box from the supermarket that had apples or oranges in it. Remember to make more than one of each mobile if you are using a big box.

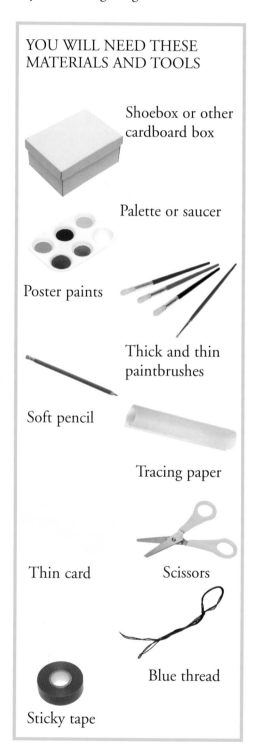

YOU WILL NEED THESE MATERIALS AND TOOLS

Shoebox or other cardboard box

Palette or saucer

Poster paints

Thick and thin paintbrushes

Soft pencil

Tracing paper

Thin card

Scissors

Blue thread

Sticky tape

1 Paint the shoebox inside and out using blue paint. You don't need the lid so don't bother with that. Leave the box to dry, then stand it on a wipe-clean surface, inside a cardboard box, or on a surface covered with newspaper.

2 Dip a medium-sized paintbrush in one of your pots of poster paint and flick the paint into the box. For fine splatters, tap the brush handle on the edge of the box. Repeat this with the different coloured paints.

3 Leave the box to dry thoroughly while you make the mobiles and decorations. Using a soft pencil, trace the star, planet and rocket templates from the beginning of the book on to pieces of card.

4 Cut out the shapes. If your box is large, you will need more than one of each. You will also need some stars for the outside of the box.

5 Cover your work surface with scrap paper, then paint each shape. Choose yellow, gold or silver for the stars and bright colours for the planet and rocket.

6 Use a piece of sticky tape to attach a length of blue thread to the shapes to hang inside the box. Glue some of the stars to the top and sides of the box.

7 Use sticky tape to attach the rocket and planet to the roof of the box.

Your own space scene will amaze your friends.

I Can Experiment

Introduction

Children are very curious people. So are scientists. Both ask questions about the world around them. How does this work? What does that do? Why do things happen? And can things be improved? You may already ask grown-ups how things happen. What, where, when and why? This means you are already a natural scientist. Scientists find the answers to their questions by doing experiments. You can do the same. This chapter shows you how to do tests and experiments for yourself. Then you can find

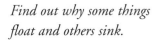

Find out why some things float and others sink.

out the answers to your questions, like a real scientist. You can also go on to invent more experiments and do more projects. Perhaps you will make a great discovery and become famous!

Young Scientists

You have already been doing experiments for years, probably without knowing it. When you were a tiny baby, you started to move your arms and legs about. You grabbed and kicked things,

Make a sound gun with a cardboard tube and discover how sound travels.

to see what would happen. When you were bigger, you probably did experiments when you played with your toys. Could you eat them? Did they make a noise when you dropped them? Could you pull them apart to see inside? Playing is experimenting, and playing is fun, so experimenting is fun, too.

Find out why things look back-to-front in a mirror.

As you do the experiments in this chapter, you will find out about light and electricity, how water and wind work, and how heat and cold affect things. Each project tells you what to do and then explains what happens. All these experiments are safe with the help of grown-ups. You can also make up your own experiments and find things out for yourself. In this way you will learn more about the world.

Different Kinds of Science

Science is so huge that no one can know everything about it.

So scientists usually specialize. This means they study just one or a few subjects. For example, medical scientists study why people become ill, and how to make them better. Biologists study animals and plants, where they live and how they grow. Chemists study chemicals and other substances, what they are made of, and how they can be changed and used. Physicists study how things move, what holds them together or pulls them apart, and how energy makes things happen. Astronomers study the planets, stars and the whole universe.

How to Do an Experiment

Whatever scientists study, they usually work in the same way. This is called the scientific method. They do not rush, and they always keep things clean and safe.

• First the scientist finds out as much as possible about the subject. This is called research. What is already known about the subject? What experiments have other scientists done, and what did they discover? Do people really know the facts, or are they just guessing?

• Then the scientist decides on a good question to ask. It should be a new question that no one has asked before. But it must not be too complicated. Most scientists find out more by working in small stages, bit by bit.

• The scientist may have an idea of the possible answer to the question. In other words, he or she may guess what will happen in the experiment. This possible answer is called a theory.

• Next, the scientist thinks of an experiment that will test the theory, to find the answer to the question. This is called planning or designing the experiment. In a good experiment, everything happens clearly and safely, and nothing can go wrong – hopefully!

• Now the scientist gathers all the bits and pieces to do the experiment. These are called the materials and equipment. Everything is set out neatly and cleanly, and labelled clearly, so that there are no mix-ups.

• At last, the scientist carries out the experiment, working carefully and safely. He or she finds out what happens by looking and listening, and perhaps by feeling or smelling. The things that happen are called the results. These are written down carefully in the Science Record Book. Everything is cleaned up and tidied away afterwards.

• Next, the scientist thinks about the results. Were they expected, or not? Is the theory right, or wrong? If the theory is right, the scientist has found something new. If the theory is wrong, the scientist can try to think of another theory, or perhaps the experiment did not work properly. Remember – no experiment is a failure. A good scientist can always learn from the results, whatever they are.

• After more experiments, the scientist will be able to gather the answers together. He or she must check everything, then check it again. Finally, the scientist may make a new discovery, and become famous.

Being a Good Scientist

Scientists are very careful people. They have to be. They often work with dangerous machines, equipment and chemicals. And science can be very costly. So scientists also need to be sure that their experiments are worthwhile, and that there will be no mistakes. So they make sure everything is thought out and prepared carefully.

When you do experiments, get the materials and equipment ready first. Have a clean, safe area to carry out your experiment in, as described over the page. And ask a grown-up to check that everything is safe.

Water is great fun to splash around, as long as you are working in a waterproof area.
Science tip For experiments with water or other liquids, see if you can do them in a large bowl, such as a washing-up bowl. This catches any splashes or spills.

Heat can be very dangerous. Hot water and steam can burn or scald your skin. And when very hot water is poured into cold jars, beakers or bowls, it can make them crack or melt. So *always* get a grown-up to help you with experiments that need hot water, and make sure your equipment can stand up to it. Cookers and kettles must only be used when a grown-up is present. Liquids can boil over suddenly, and things may catch fire without warning.

Put a metal teaspoon into a jar before pouring in hot water.

Use a jug with a spout and a funnel when pouring liquids.

Never touch electric sockets, plugs or wires.

Wear a pair of rubber gloves when handling vinegar or lemon juice.

Always ask a grown-up to cut anything with sharp scissors or a craft knife.

Science tip Put a metal teaspoon into a jar before pouring in hot water. This should stop the heat cracking the jar.

Ice can freeze skin just as badly as hot water can burn. Ice has the added danger that it sticks to dry skin. When you make ice in a freezer, get a grown-up to help you.
Science tip Use rubber or washing-up gloves when handling ice. Wet the ice and the gloves first, so they do not stick together.

Electricity from a small battery is usually safe, since there is not enough power to give a shock. Static electricity can sometimes be felt as a tingle that makes you jump, for example when it builds up on a car and you touch the handle. But the static that builds up on a balloon, as shown in one of the experiments, is too small to feel.
Science tip The electricity that is used in the home is very dangerous. It can kill! NEVER touch electric sockets, plugs or wires.

Chemicals used here are mostly substances used for cooking and they are harmless in normal quantities. But good scientists know that chemicals can be dangerous if they get into the wrong place. This includes near too much heat, or inside your body if you swallow them. Never taste or eat chemicals that you are using for experiments. Always ask a grown-up to get the things you need from the kitchen cupboard. NEVER touch cleaning chemicals, medicines or alcohol.

Science tip Use rubber gloves to handle large quantities of acids like vinegar or lemon juice.

Cutting

and making holes can be quite difficult. Scissors and sharp points can be dangerous if they are not used properly. So ask a grown-up to help.

Science tip Draw a line where you are going to cut with scissors, before you start cutting. It is usually easier to follow a line.

Label everything

– it is the sign of a good scientist. Your experiment might be ruined if you cannot remember what you put in each jar, or if you get your chemicals mixed up. Write labels on pieces of paper or use special sticky-backed labels. Stick these in the right place, or put them under jars or beakers.

Science tip Use a pencil for your labels. Some felt-tipped pens can blot and run if splashed with water.

Your Science Record Book

All scientists record their experiments and the results. You need to know exactly what you did during an experiment, so that you can repeat it to check the result, or change it to find out something else. Each time you do an experiment, record the following information in your book. If you find writing difficult ask a grown-up to help with some of the details and draw a picture of what happened instead.

- the day and date
- the experiment's name, and the idea behind it
- how you did your experiment, perhaps with a drawing or diagram
- the results, written in words, or perhaps as a chart with ticks and crosses

You can make a Science Record Book by covering a notebook or school-type exercise book with coloured paper. The paper needs to be about 3–4 cm (1¼–1½ in) larger all around than the book when it is opened flat.

Further Research

When scientists have finished their set of experiments, they often try to find out a bit more, perhaps by changing the experiment slightly. See if you can make changes to some of your experiments to find out more. Record what you do and your results in your Science Record Book.

Your Science Record Book

1 Place the book centrally on the coloured paper, with one cover open. Turn the edges of the paper over the cover and stick them down with glue. You can snip the corners of the paper to give a neater finish. Repeat with the other cover.

2 Decorate the cover with something scientific, perhaps numbers, bubbles and shapes, drawings of test-tubes and scientific equipment, or cut-out photographs of scientific gadgets.

3 Record all the information that you have learned from your experiments. If you like, you can stick some of the things you have made in the book, to keep.

Where to Do Experiments

Many scientists work in special rooms called laboratories. There they have all the equipment, materials, tools and machines they need to do their experiments. But not all science happens in laboratories. To do research, many scientists go to libraries to read books. They visit exhibitions and museums to find out more. They also meet other scientists and talk about their work.

The Home Laboratory

You can set up your own laboratory in your home or school. It might be in a kitchen, bathroom, shed or garage. You usually need somewhere with waterproof surfaces, where there is no danger of damaging furniture or carpets. Ask a grown-up to choose the best place.

The main thing you will need is a large work surface, like a table. The place should be brightly lit and not too hot or cold. For some experiments, you will need a freezer, or a refrigerator with a freezing compartment. You will sometimes need lots of water. Warm water can come from a hot tap or a kettle. You might also need somewhere to heat up a saucepan. Always ask a grown-up to help.

Science tip Cover your work surface with several layers of old newspaper. This stops paint and food colouring staining the work surface, and will also absorb spilt liquids and glue.

Materials and Equipment

You will find most of the materials, equipment and tools that you need for your experiments around the house. Always gather everything you need and check it before you start the experiment. If you do not, you may run out of something halfway through.

If necessary, you can buy extra supplies of pencils, pens, scissors, sticky tape, paper, card, blotting paper, glue, sticky labels and shapes, poster paints and similar things from a good stationery shop or office supplier.

You can find food colourings, bicarbonate of soda, vinegar, lemon juice, milk, cocktail sticks, skewers and similar things in the kitchen.

Batteries, wires and small torch bulbs are sold in electrical, DIY or model shops. You can buy small mirrors from the chemist, and sand or gravel from a builders' supplier or a timber merchant.

Be a Green Scientist

Good scientists know that they must look after our planet by saving resources, recycling things, and not damaging the environment or causing waste and pollution. This is called being "green" since it helps to save trees, plants, flowers, animals and natural places on our planet Earth.

You can be a "green scientist" by saving, reusing and recycling things. You will also save money!

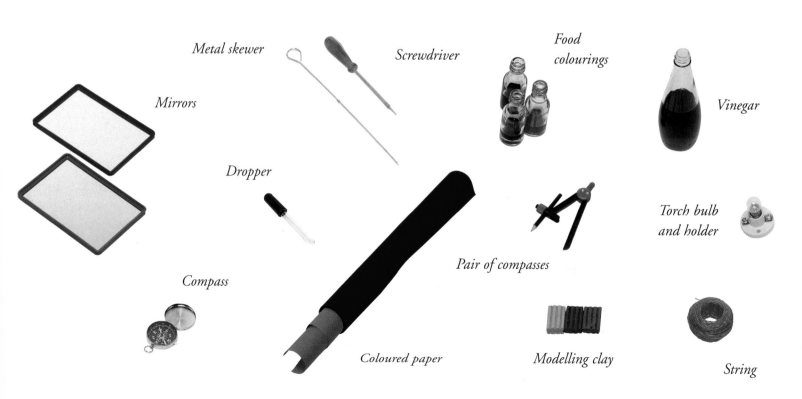

Metal skewer

Screwdriver

Food colourings

Mirrors

Vinegar

Dropper

Torch bulb and holder

Pair of compasses

Compass

Coloured paper

Modelling clay

String

Plastic strainer

Bottle

Tissue paper

9-volt battery

Jars

Plastic cups

Balloons

Coloured stickers

Sand

Electrical wire

Bicarbonate of soda

• Use old newspapers, and store your equipment in empty cartons or boxes.
• The card from cereal boxes is ideal for many experiments.
• Ask grown-ups for used paper that has been written on one side – you can use the blank side.
• After picnics and parties, wash the paper or plastic cups and plates. You can use them for your experiments.
• Save the cardboard tubes from the insides of toilet rolls and kitchen rolls.
• Wash and keep empty jars for your experiments. But remember that glass is easily broken and is then very dangerous to handle.
• Save plastic drinks bottles. Carefully cut off the tops and turn them upside-down to make funnels. The lower parts make plastic jars – safer than glass ones.
• When you have finished with your equipment, take it to your local recycling centre.

Have Fun

If you follow the safety rules in this book, and carry out your experiments slowly and sensibly, you will find that science is fun. You can make some amazing discoveries, and learn lots.

Find out more by doing further research, by reading about science, and by watching science programmes. You can become an expert scientist and answer all your friends' questions. You might even make a discovery or invention that will change the world!

A Note for Grown-ups

Some of the experiments in this book can be followed by a child alone, but often adult help is needed. Always supervise your children closely whenever they are using home experiment materials. The places in the book where your assistance is vital, such as when sharp scissors or a craft knife are needed, are marked !.

Creatures of the Night

Light is bright, and when there is no light it is dark. A shadow is a patch of darkness. It is formed when something gets in the way of light beams, which can only travel in straight lines. In Alex's puppet show, some of the light from the torch shines on the wall. But the light that hits the ghostly black creatures cannot get through or round them. So the wall behind their shapes stays dark – as their shady, scary shadows.

You can make the shadows on the wall bigger or smaller. When the puppets are near the torch, they cover more of the light beam, and so the shadows on the wall are bigger, but their edges are fuzzy and blurred.

Light fantastic

Light is amazing. It comes and goes in a flash, weighs nothing, travels faster than anything else in the universe – and even scientists do not fully understand it. The light we turn on in our homes is produced by electricity. This passes through the very thin wire inside a light bulb and makes the wire glow brightly. The light beams then spread out in all directions, and always in straight lines. The light bulb in a torch has a mirror behind it to make all the light beams come out at the front only.

! Young children will need help cutting out card shapes with scissors and should not be allowed to handle craft knives. They might also need help in the "dark room", to hold the torch or just for company. Be sure they cannot get themselves locked in a dark room or cupboard.

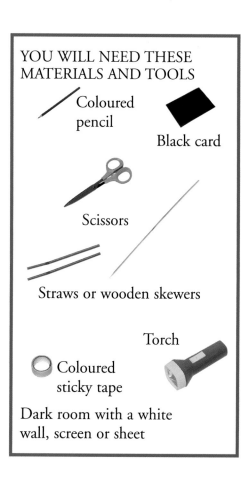

YOU WILL NEED THESE MATERIALS AND TOOLS

Coloured pencil

Black card

Scissors

Straws or wooden skewers

Torch

Coloured sticky tape

Dark room with a white wall, screen or sheet

1 Draw the outlines of some night-time creatures, like bats, owls and spiders, on the black card with the pencil. Make them big.

2 Draw some stars and a moon too. Cut out the shapes carefully with scissors. If the scissors are sharp, ask a grown-up to help you.

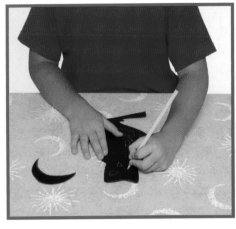

3 Draw features such as eyes and feathers or even bone patterns onto the night-time creatures. Keep these quite simple.

4 Ask a grown-up to cut out the eyes, feather patterns and any other details with a craft knife.

5 Stick the straws or skewers to the shapes with sticky tape to make handles.

Changing Shadows

Things that light can pass through easily, like air or glass, are called **transparent.** Solid things like your night creature cut-outs do not let any light pass through. They are **opaque.** A **translucent** substance is one that lets through some light but not all of it, like tracing paper or tissue paper. Cover one side of a cut-out animal with tissue paper. When you hold it up in front of the torch, less light will shine through the holes.

6 In a darkened room, ask a friend to shine the torch on a light wall. Move the creatures and other shapes in the torch's light, to make their ghostly shadows dance on the wall.

Mysterious Mirrors

Otis is discovering that what you see in a mirror is not an exact copy of the original thing. It is back-to-front – a mirror picture or mirror-image. His drawings and writing always look the other way round in the mirror. So does your face! The face that you see when you look in the mirror is a mirror-image. It is not the same as the face that your friends and family see when they look at you, or when you look at a photograph of yourself.

Reflections

Light beams travel in straight lines – unless they bounce off things. This bouncing is called **reflection.** Only a few things, like the Sun, light bulbs, candles and fires, give out their own light beams. These shine into our eyes and we see them. We see other things because they bounce or reflect light beams into our eyes. Very smooth, shiny surfaces like mirrors are very good at reflecting. When you look at your face in a mirror, you see light beams that have come from the Sun or an electric light to your face, bounced off it towards the mirror, and then bounced back again into your eyes!

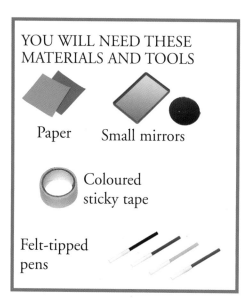

YOU WILL NEED THESE
MATERIALS AND TOOLS

Paper   Small mirrors

Coloured
sticky tape

Felt-tipped
pens

Otis is having fun making his drawings and writing turn around in a mirror. See if you can make a mirror-image come out the right way round.

1 Mirrors are made of glass or plastic. Some may have sharp edges. Ask a grown-up to put some sticky tape round them to make them safe.

2 Do a drawing and write the name of what you have drawn on a piece of paper. Be as neat as you can.

3 Hold the mirror up next to the paper. Can you read the writing in it? Does the drawing look exactly the same as it does on the paper?

4 Write the name backwards or do the drawing back-to-front. What does it look like in the mirror now?

5 Think of a whole drawing. Draw half of it, using one half of the paper only.

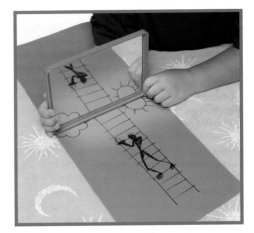

6 Can you make up the rest of the drawing by holding the mirror alongside it? Is the result what you had expected?

See Back to the Future!

You can make an image bounce backwards and forwards between mirrors, almost for ever. Sit behind one mirror. Hold out another mirror facing you. Look into this mirror. Move both mirrors slightly until you can see the reflection of the mirror in the reflection of the mirror in the reflection of the mirror in the reflection of the mirror and on and on.

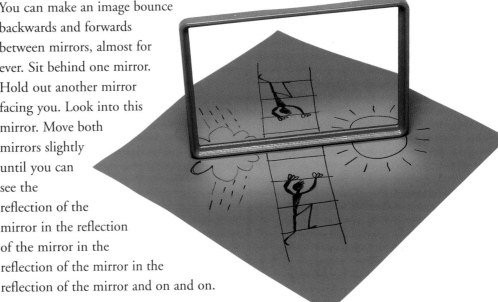

Battery Light Show

Kirsty has made a light show, to demonstrate how electricity works. Electricity is stored in the battery. It can only move, or flow, when it has a complete circle, or circuit, to go around. This circuit is made from wires, a switch and a bulb. When the switch is ON, the electricity goes from one end, or terminal, on the battery, along the wires, through the switch and light bulb, back to the battery's other terminal. As electricity goes through the bulb, it glows. When the switch is OFF, it makes a gap or break in the circuit. The electricity stops – and the light goes out.

Electric likes and dislikes

Electricity flows easily through some materials, like metals such as steel, iron and copper, and also water. These are called **conductors.** Electricity cannot flow through other things, like plastic, wood and pottery. These are called **insulators.** The wires in this experiment are made of metal on the inside, so the electricity can flow. The wire is covered with plastic to stop the electricity escaping.

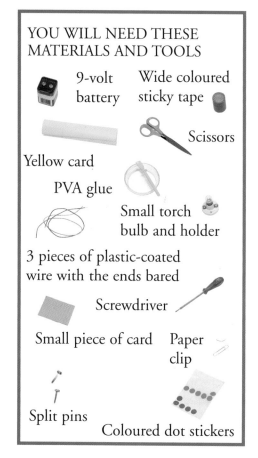

YOU WILL NEED THESE MATERIALS AND TOOLS

9-volt battery

Wide coloured sticky tape

Scissors

Yellow card

PVA glue

Small torch bulb and holder

3 pieces of plastic-coated wire with the ends bared

Screwdriver

Small piece of card

Paper clip

Split pins

Coloured dot stickers

A 9-volt battery is perfectly safe for doing experiments. A grown-up should strip about 1 cm (1/2 in) of plastic from both ends of each piece of wire. Be careful how you screw the light bulb into its holder, since too much force may break the glass. Young children might need help with screws and screwdrivers.

W A R N I N G
NEVER TOUCH ELECTRICAL WIRES, SWITCHES, PLUGS OR SOCKETS WITHOUT HELP FROM A GROWN-UP.

Kirsty switches the light on and off, showing how she can start and stop the electricity going around the circuit.

1 Decorate the battery to make it look powerful by winding a piece of wide coloured sticky tape right around it.

2 Cut out some zig-zag "lightning flashes" from the yellow card and stick them onto the sides of the battery with glue.

3 Screw the light bulb into the holder. Push the end of a piece of wire under one of the connecting screws. Screw it down. Repeat with another piece of wire under the other screw.

4 Take the end of one of these pieces of wire and twist it onto one of the battery terminals (the bits of metal on the top of the battery).

5 Twist the end of the third piece of wire onto the other battery terminal. Make sure that both these wires grip the terminals tightly.

7 Twist one free wire end around one split pin and the other around the other split pin. When the paper clip touches both split pins, the switch is ON (green dot) and the light bulb shines. When the paper clip is moved away from the split pin, the switch is OFF (red dot).

6 Push two holes in the piece of card, the length of the paper clip apart. Push a split pin through one hole. Push the other split pin through the paper clip and then through the other hole. Open the ends of the pins under the card. This is the switch.

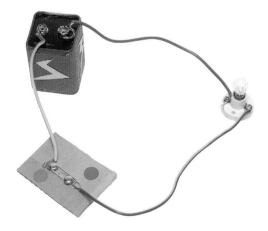

Tumbler Telephone

Can you talk to a friend quietly, when he or she is at the other end of a big room? Liam's telephone works by sending the sound waves of his voice along the string. They go along the string as very fast to-and-fro movements called vibrations. When Liam talks into the tumbler or cup, the sound waves hit the bottom of the tumbler and make it vibrate.

The vibrations pass along the string to the tumbler at the other end. They shake the bottom of this tumbler, which makes sound waves that go into Lorenzo's ear.

With his own tumbler telephone, Liam never gets a wrong number, and the lines are never busy. Also, his calls are always free!

Travelling waves

Sound waves travel well through air. They go through lots of other things too, such as water, wood, metals and glass. In fact, sound travels much faster and farther as vibrations in water, metals and glass, than it does through air. This is why whales and dolphins can "talk" to each other across huge distances in the ocean.

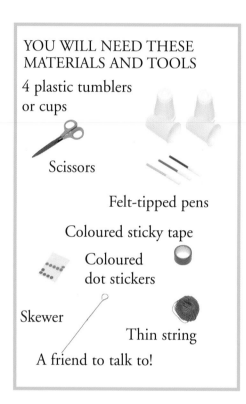

YOU WILL NEED THESE MATERIALS AND TOOLS

4 plastic tumblers or cups

Scissors

Felt-tipped pens

Coloured sticky tape

Coloured dot stickers

Skewer

Thin string

A friend to talk to!

! The tumbler telephone works well if the string is stretched quite tight and straight, and nothing touches it. Otherwise the vibrations cannot travel along it properly. The tumblers should be held by their rims only, so the bottoms are free to vibrate. Children may need help with cutting the tumblers and making holes with a sharp point.

1 Carefully cut the bottoms off two of the tumblers about 2 cm (¾ in) from the base. You may need to ask a grown-up to help you with this.

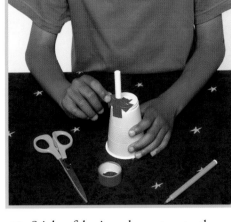

2 Stick a felt-tipped pen top to the bottom of each of the other two tumblers. These will be "aerials" – your telephones are like mobile ones!

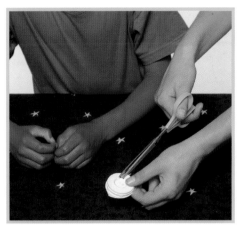

3 Ask a grown-up to cut out small holes in the cut-off tumbler bottoms. Slip them neatly over the "aerials" to hold them in place.

4 Sticky-tape the cut-off bottoms in place. Add more stripes of sticky tape for decoration.

5 Make a "key pad" on each telephone with coloured dot stickers. Write numbers on the dots.

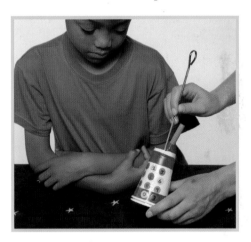

6 Ask a grown-up to make a tiny hole in the bottoms of the tumblers, with a skewer.

7 Thread the ends of the string through the holes in the telephones. Tie a large knot in each end of the string.

Chatting on the Telephone

Your friend walks away with one of the tumbler telephones, until the string is stretched tight, and holds the telephone to his or her ear. You speak into the telephone, and your friend listens. When you have finished talking, say "Over" like a real walkie-talkie user. Hold the telephone to your ear, to hear your friend's reply. Try using longer string to see if the telephone still works. Measure the greatest length and write the results in your Science Record Book.

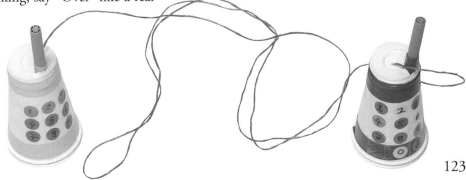

Marvellous Mobiles

Air is all around us. We can not see it or touch it. But when it moves, we can feel it. Moving air comes from your mouth when you blow, and from a fan. The wind is moving air. Stand outside on a windy day and sometimes the moving air nearly knocks you over. Antonino's marvellous mobile swirls and twirls when moving air pushes it. You can find moving air around the house, such as near a window, door, radiator or table lamp.

Rising air

Indoors, moving air is sometimes called a draught, especially when it is cold and unwanted. Draughts in houses are caused by the wind blowing through gaps around windows or doors. Draughts are also caused in other ways. Hot air from a radiator or table lamp rises up to the ceiling, and makes a warm draught. On a cold night, cold air near a window falls to the floor as a cold draught.

Children may need help with cutting and balancing the mobile. Hanging the mobile near any heat source, such as a radiator or lamp, must be supervised.

Antonino can use his marvellous mobile to detect wind, draughts and other moving air in his house.

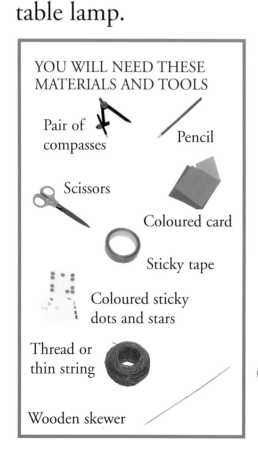

YOU WILL NEED THESE MATERIALS AND TOOLS

Pair of compasses

Pencil

Scissors

Coloured card

Sticky tape

Coloured sticky dots and stars

Thread or thin string

Wooden skewer

1 Use the compasses to draw lots of circles on the coloured card. Make them any size but there must be two of each size.

2 Carefully cut out the circles using scissors. Arrange the discs in their equal-sized pairs.

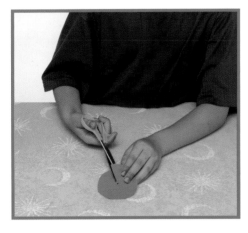

3 Carefully cut a straight line or slit from the edge of each disc to its centre, where the compass point was.

4 Push the two discs of each pair together by their slits. Secure the joins with some sticky tape to make sure they hold together.

5 Decorate the discs with the coloured dots and stars.

6 Cut the string or thread into different lengths. Stick one end of a string to the centre of each pair of discs. Tie the other end to the skewer.

A Mobile Draught-detector

Balance the mobile by moving the strings along the skewer until it does not tip over. Now, find places around the house where you can hang the mobile. If it turns or wobbles, you know there is air moving past it. Make a list of the places you test in your Science Record Book. Can you think what might cause the draughts?

Above: Tie another length of string to the centre of the skewer so you can hang it up.

Hold Water Upside Down!

This famous trick looks impossible, or perhaps it is magic. Can you really hold water in an upside-down tumbler? Yes, Antonino shows that it truly does work. It depends on science. The force that pulls you, a cat, a chair and everything else in the world, down towards the ground, is called gravity. Gravity tries to make the water fall out of the upside-down tumbler towards the ground. But in this trick, air keeps the water in the tumbler.

Heavy air

Air has weight, although it does not weigh much. There is a lot of it pressing on us, since there is a huge amount of air high above. We do not notice this pressing force, because we are used to it. It is called **air pressure**, and it is this that keeps the water in the glass. The water is trapped inside the glass by the card. Air presses down, around and up underneath the card, holding it in place, and keeping the water inside the tumbler.

YOU WILL NEED THESE MATERIALS AND TOOLS

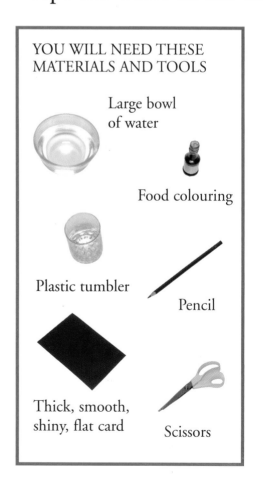

Large bowl of water

Food colouring

Plastic tumbler

Pencil

Thick, smooth, shiny, flat card

Scissors

This experiment involves a lot of water and does not always work right first time. So it should be performed in a suitable waterproof area. Use a plastic tumbler and bowl rather than glass ones, for safety. We have used glass ones here so you can see how the experiment works. Clean, smooth, shiny, flat card is best. The experiment works less well if the card becomes soggy or bent. Children may need help cutting the card.

It looks like magic. But Antonino is using the science of air, water and gravity to stop his feet getting wet!

1 Add a little food colouring to the water in the bowl and stir it around. This is so you can see the water inside the tumbler.

2 Draw around the rim of the tumbler onto the card. Then draw a square around this circle, about 2 cm (3/4 in) larger than the circle all around.

3 Carefully cut out the square of card. It should fit easily over the top of the tumbler, with plenty of extra card around the rim.

4 Put the tumbler into the bowl of water. Hold it under, with the open end pointing up. Make sure that it fills up completely.

5 Make sure there are no bubbles of air inside the tumbler, by tapping it. The trick will not work if there is any air in the tumbler.

6 Turn the tumbler upside down. Lift it partly out, but keep the rim under the water. Slide the card into the water and under the rim.

7 Hold the card firmly against the rim of the beaker. Slowly lift the card and beaker, still upside down, out of the water.

8 Hold the tumbler upside down and level. Without sliding the card, take your other hand away from the card.

Air, Water and Weather

The layer of air all around the Earth is called the atmosphere. Air's weight changes when it gets hot or cold, and these changes cause our weather. When air is warmed by the sun, it rises higher. Cooler air moves along to take its place. This is wind. As air rises, the invisible moisture in it turns to tiny drops of water. These make clouds. As the drops get bigger, they fall as rain.

Sink or Swim

Water is very strong. It can push things. When it flows in rivers, or in sea currents, it pushes objects along. Water also pushes down all the time, because it is very heavy. But it also pushes up, too. This upwards pushing is called upthrust, and it makes things float. Izabella is discovering that water's upthrust is strong enough to support some things and make them float, but that others are too heavy and sink.

Do not use glass or sharp objects in this experiment. A suitable waterproof area is essential.

Izabella tests some household things to see if they sink or float in water. You could try lots of other objects too.

Floating forces

An object floats if the upwards push of the water, called **upthrust,** is more than the downwards push of the object. The downwards push of the object is called **displacement** because it moves aside (dis-places) some water. An object that is small for its weight, like a pebble, displaces only a small amount of water. So it sinks. If an object is large for its weight, like a sponge, it floats.

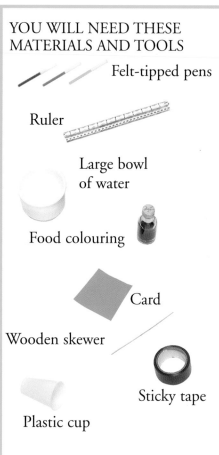

YOU WILL NEED THESE MATERIALS AND TOOLS

Felt-tipped pens

Ruler

Large bowl of water

Food colouring

Card

Wooden skewer

Sticky tape

Plastic cup

Household items or toys like a cork, pumice stone, pebble, small sieve, metal dish, clothes peg, dry sponge, paper clip, wooden spoon, metal spoon, nail, piece of polystyrene, table-tennis ball, and so on.

1 Draw a chart in your Science Record Book with three columns. In the first column, write the names or draw the items you will test. The middle column is for those that SWIM. The last is for those that SINK.

2 Ask a grown-up to fill a large bowl of water. Stir in some food colouring – just for fun!

3 Make a float-marker by cutting out a sail shape from the piece of card. Tape it to a wooden skewer. Ask a grown up to push the skewer into the bottom of a plastic cup. Half-fill the cup with water and float it.

4 Put the cork, the pumice stone and the pebble on the surface of the water. Do they sink or swim?

5 Put a cross in the SINK or a tick in the SWIM column of your Science Record Book for each item.

6 Try to float the small sieve and the metal dish. Put the results in your Science Record Book.

7 Test a clothes peg and the sponge. Leave the sponge in the water for a long time. Does it still float as high?

Weight, Shape and Water

If something has air in it, like the dry sponge, it weighs less. So it is likely to float. The metal dish also has air "in" it when it is the right way up, so it floats too. This is how metal boats float. If the air is replaced by water, the object becomes heavier and it may sink. This is why the sponge gradually floats lower as it soaks up water. Tip over the dish and it fills with water and sinks. This is what happens when a boat capsizes. The float-marker is half full of water and half full of air, so it half floats. Pumice stone is bubbly rock full of air that is made by volcanoes.

The Great Iceberg Puzzle

One of the great puzzles of nature is how icebergs float. Icebergs are huge lumps of ice that drift about in the cold seas near the North and South Poles. Some icebergs are bigger than cities. They weigh thousands of tonnes. As water gets colder, it gets heavier. So cold water sinks below warm water. Icebergs are frozen water and so are even colder. So why do they not sink to the bottom of the sea? Lorenzo finds out why in this experiment, by using tiny icebergs from a refrigerator or freezer. They will work the same as a real iceberg, but they are much smaller!

Lorenzo has made lots of coloured "icebergs". He is investigating how they float and then melt.

YOU WILL NEED THESE MATERIALS AND TOOLS

A large see-through bowl of warm water

Ice-cube tray

Food colourings

Jug

Plastic paint pots or jars

Spoon

Light ice

As water gets colder, it becomes heavier. But this only happens down to the temperature of 4°C (40°F). If it gets colder than that, it begins to get lighter again and so rises towards the surface. When it cools to 0°C (32°F), liquid water freezes into solid ice. This cold ice is quite light and it floats on water. This means that animals and plants which live in water do not have to freeze solid themselves when the temperature drops to or below freezing. They can survive in the cold water below the ice that floats on ponds and lakes.

1 Make some mini-icebergs by putting food colouring into some water in paint pots or jars. You can make them in several different colours, but do not mix the colours together.

2 Spoon the coloured water carefully into the ice-cube tray or other containers, if you wish. Put this into a freezer or the freezing compartment of a refrigerator. Leave until frozen solid.

3 When the ice-cubes are frozen, fill the large bowl with warm water. Ask a grown-up to help you with this. Then remove the ice-cube tray from the freezer or refrigerator.

4 Drop coloured ice-cubes into the water. Watch what happens. Do they sink? Look at the bowl from the side. Can you see the ice melting? What does it do?

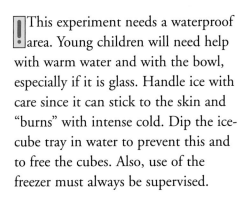

This experiment needs a waterproof area. Young children will need help with warm water and with the bowl, especially if it is glass. Handle ice with care since it can stick to the skin and "burns" with intense cold. Dip the ice-cube tray in water to prevent this and to free the cubes. Also, use of the freezer must always be supervised.

Underwater Fountain

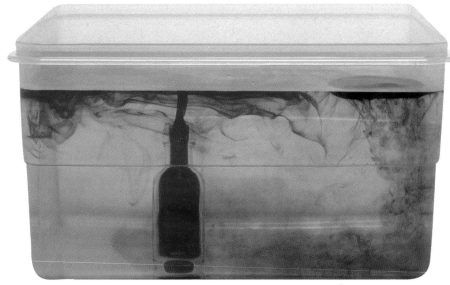

You can investigate how warm water floats and cold water sinks by making an underwater fountain. Fill a large bowl with cold water. Then fill a small plastic bottle with warm water. (The plastic bottle must be small enough to sink below the surface of the water in the bowl.) Add some food colouring to it. Carefully lower the bottle into the bowl and make it sit on the bottom. Does the warm coloured water stay in the bottle? Where does it go? Draw a picture of your fountain in your Science Research Book to show your results. You could also try dropping in some coloured ice-cubes, made with a different food colouring, into the water. The ice is lighter than the water around it, so it floats. The warmer water melts the coloured ice. But the coloured water that comes from the ice is colder and heavier than the water, so it sinks. Look very carefully to see the cold, coloured water trickling from the iceberg and sinking to the bottom.

Kitchen Chemistry

Everything in the world is made of chemicals. Some are artificial chemicals, like those made in factories. Others are natural chemicals, like those in your own body and in the rocks and soil. Even the food you eat is made of chemicals. Scientists who study chemicals are called chemists. You can be a kitchen chemist, like Dean, and study the chemicals in the cupboard. Cooking is a form of chemistry. You mix together the chemicals and make them join together, or react, to form a tasty snack.

The acid test

Some cooking substances, like vinegar or lemon juice, are sour. They are called **acidic.** Other kitchen substances, like bicarbonate of soda (bicarb), are slightly slimy and bitter. They are called **basic** or **alkali.** Bases are the opposite of acids. Chemists often need to know whether chemicals are acids or bases. If they do not know what the chemicals are, they should never taste them to find out, because many chemicals are poisonous. So chemists make special substances called **chemical indicators,** to test them. Red cabbage water is a good chemical indicator to tell the difference between acids and bases.

Young children must be supervised in the kitchen, as some foods and liquids can cause sickness in large quantities. Chopping and boiling the cabbage should always be done by a grown-up.

Dean has put a strip of blotting paper into each of his test jars. The name of the test juice or liquid is marked on the paper in pencil. He can then let the strips dry and clip them into his Science Record Book.

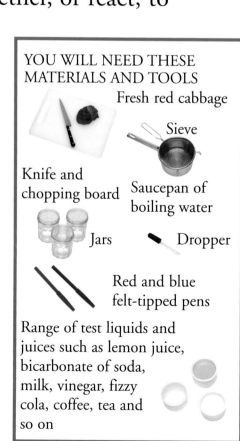

YOU WILL NEED THESE MATERIALS AND TOOLS

Fresh red cabbage

Sieve

Knife and chopping board

Saucepan of boiling water

Jars

Dropper

Red and blue felt-tipped pens

Range of test liquids and juices such as lemon juice, bicarbonate of soda, milk, vinegar, fizzy cola, coffee, tea and so on

1 Ask a grown-up to chop the cabbage, put it into boiling water for about 15 minutes, then strain the water through a sieve.

2 While the chemical indicator (the red cabbage water) is cooling, put a little tap water into each jar. Get your Science Record Book ready.

3 Add about 15 drops of the chemical indicator to each jar, using the dropper. Look at the colour and note it in your Science Record Book.

4 Add one test liquid to a jar, such as a spoonful of juice squeezed from a lemon. Stir it in. Watch and note down any colour change.

5 Add another test liquid, such as a spoonful of milk, to the next jar. As before, mix it, and note down any colour change in your book.

Recording Your Results

Colour in the result of each experiment in your Science Record Book. Draw three columns. In the first column, write the name or draw a picture of the test substance. In the second column put a mark for those that turned red or orange with a red felt-tipped pen. In the third column put a mark for those that turned purple or blue with a blue felt-tipped pen. Acids join or react with the red cabbage water to turn it red or orange. Bases do the same but turn it purple or blue. During the experiment, keep one jar that contains just the chemical indicator. Scientists call this a "control". You can compare the colour changes in the other jars with the original colour in the "control" jar.

6 Add the next test liquid, such as a few drops of vinegar, to the next jar. Note any change. Do this with the other test liquids and juices.

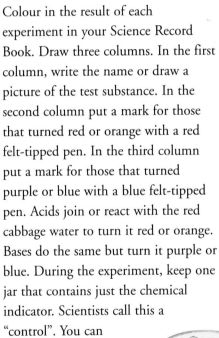

Vinegar Volcano

What happens when acids and bases, or alkalis, meet? Kirsty has made a peaceful-looking tropical island, but it is about to get shaken by a huge volcano. She can make the volcano explode or erupt using simple chemicals – the acid vinegar and the base bicarbonate of soda. The spectacular effect is caused by the reaction between the acid and the base. The food colouring makes it look like real, red-hot, runny rock.

YOU WILL NEED THESE MATERIALS AND TOOLS

Red food colouring

Vinegar

2 small plastic or glass bottles

Funnel

Bicarbonate of soda (bicarb)

Large blue plate

Sand

PVA glue

Coloured paper

Pencil

Scissors

Coloured sticky tape

Fizzy gas

Everything is made of chemicals. And all chemicals are made of tiny particles called **atoms.** During a chemical reaction, the groups of atoms are taken apart, mixed and shuffled, then joined together in different groups, to make new chemicals. When vinegar is mixed with bicarbonate of soda (bicarb), one of the new chemicals formed is a gas. The bubbles of this gas make the volcano fizz.

This chemical reaction is not dangerous. The gas produced is carbon dioxide, but with the recommended quantities of vinegar and bicarbonate of soda (bicarb), its amounts are very small and not harmful. However, the child should be supervised in case of spillage.

Kirsty's vinegar volcanic island is based on a simple chemical reaction. A real volcano is millions of times more powerful, and based on heat and pressure.

134

1 Add some red food colouring to some vinegar in a small bottle using the funnel.

2 Wash and dry the funnel. Use it to put 1 or 2 dessert spoons of bicarb into another small bottle.

3 Stand this bottle in the middle of the plate as the volcano. Pile the sand around it.

Lots of Eruptions

The red, bubbly "lava" fizzes out of the top of the volcano. The chemical reaction starts as soon as the vinegar mixes with the bicarb. When the volcano has finished erupting, stir inside the bottle with a skewer and pour in some more vinegar. You may get several eruptions in this way.

4 Paint the sides of the bottle with glue, to make it stick. Leave the bottle's mouth clear. This is the volcano's opening, or crater.

5 Make a palm tree. Draw some leaves on green paper and cut them out. Snip around their edges to make fronds. Roll up some coloured paper to make the tree trunk.

6 Tape round the top and bottom of the trunk and cut it off square, so it stands up. Tape the palm leaf shapes to the top of the trunk.

7 Using the funnel, carefully pour some of the coloured vinegar onto the bicarb in the bottle on the island, and quickly remove the funnel.

I Can Make Music

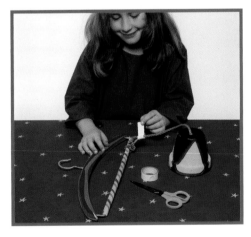

Introduction

What is music? Very simply, music is made from sounds that are pleasing or interesting to hear. Birdsong can be described as music and so can the sounds of the wind or the sea. Many people who write music – composers – have copied the sounds of nature in their music.

Sound is caused by vibrations in the air. The stronger the vibrations, the louder the sound. Musical instruments help us to make music by producing many different sounds. Your own voice is a musical instrument. See how many sounds you can make by altering the shape of your mouth, by using your tongue in different ways, and by changing the pitch of your voice from high to low. We humans are a mixture of the different types of instruments described below: we are wind instruments because we use air to make sounds; stringed instruments because we speak or sing through our vocal cords, which are like strings low down in our throats; and percussion instruments because we can clap our hands and snap our fingers.

Gabriella's bottle xylophone is a percussion instrument.

just drums that are percussion instruments. There are all kinds of fun shakers and rattles which are also used to give rhythm in music.

Wind Instruments

These are the instruments that you blow. The air vibrates inside the hollow instrument and makes a sound. The first instruments of this kind were made out of hollow animal horns or bones. Wind instruments sometimes have a "reed" to help make a good sound, and a drinking straw works very well for this.

Stringed Instruments

These instruments can be plucked with your fingers or played with a bow. The strings were first made out of hair and silk. All stringed instruments need a hollow box of some kind over which the strings are attached. The box is full of air, which vibrates when you play the instrument.

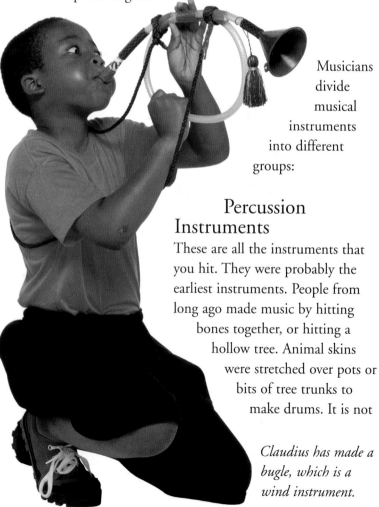

Musicians divide musical instruments into different groups:

Percussion Instruments

These are all the instruments that you hit. They were probably the earliest instruments. People from long ago made music by hitting bones together, or hitting a hollow tree. Animal skins were stretched over pots or bits of tree trunks to make drums. It is not

Claudius has made a bugle, which is a wind instrument.

This shoebox guitar is a stringed instrument. The strings are made from rubberbands.

Jessica is making a drum from a mini plastic dustbin.

Musical Families

See how many instruments you can think of and try to place them in a family or group. Is the piano a stringed instrument? It has strings but they are not plucked or played with a bow. If you look inside the piano you will see that small felt hammers hit the strings to make the sounds. It is a percussion instrument!

Making Musical Instruments

This chapter will help you to discover lots of different sounds by making your own instruments and then playing them. They are very easy to make. All you need to make music is a cardboard tube or drinks can, and a few bottle tops or a bath hat! Some of the instruments come from countries like Africa and Latin America, so it is a good chance to decorate them with really bright colours. If you make one of the fun shakers or rattles, it will feel like carnival time!

It is great fun to make music with someone else to help.

Maracas are filled with rice or beans and make a wonderful sound when shaken in the air.

Making Music Together

It is even more fun playing music in groups. Perhaps you and your friends can each make a different instrument to play. First try a rhythm game. Each of you choose a word and then play the rhythm (the beat) of that word on your instruments over and over again. Try to keep time with everyone else, then experiment by getting louder then softer, and slower then faster.

You could join in with your favourite pop song. Start with the percussion instruments to make the rhythm, then add a wind instrument like a kazoo to sing the tune. See how many different instruments you can use. Make up some music to describe a storm, a ghost story, or a trip to the zoo.

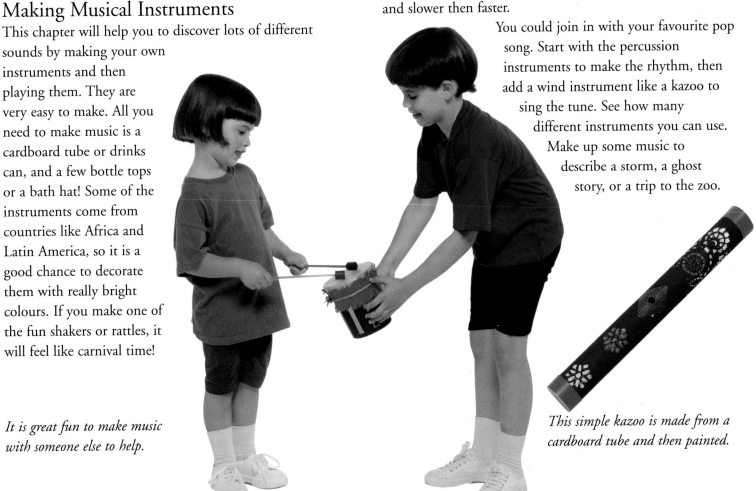

This simple kazoo is made from a cardboard tube and then painted.

Clashing Castanets

Castanets come from Spain, where they are used in flamenco dancing. The dancers stamp their feet and click their castanets in time to the music. It is very exciting to watch them. See if you can dance the same way. Izabella has made her castanets with metal pastry-cutters, so they make a wonderful sound. *Olé*!

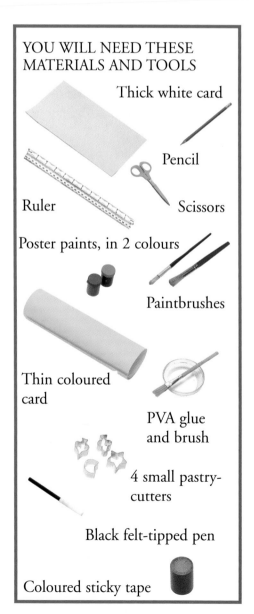

YOU WILL NEED THESE
MATERIALS AND TOOLS

Thick white card

Pencil

Ruler

Scissors

Poster paints, in 2 colours

Paintbrushes

Thin coloured card

PVA glue and brush

4 small pastry-cutters

Black felt-tipped pen

Coloured sticky tape

Making music
Clash the pastry-cutters together in time to the music. You can also play them by resting your hand on a table.

! Children may need help measuring out and cutting and scoring the card.

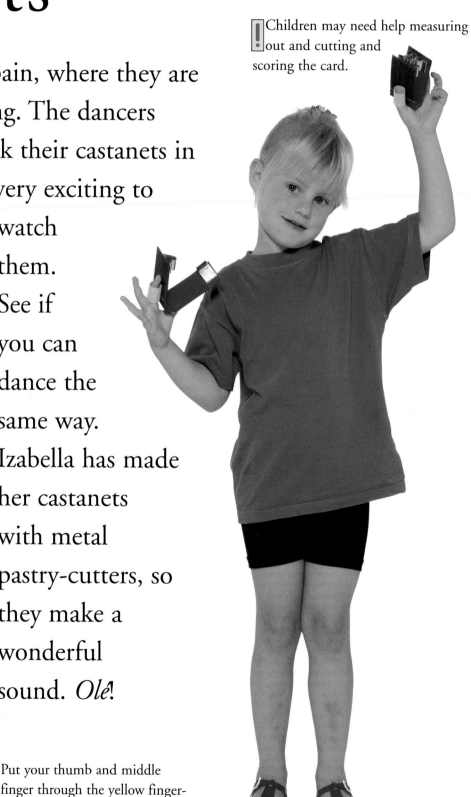

Put your thumb and middle finger through the yellow finger-holders and play away!

1 Draw a rectangle 20 cm (8 in) long and 7 cm (3 in) wide on thick white card. Draw two lines 4 cm (1½ in) apart down the centre of the rectangle.

2 Carefully cut out the rectangle. Bend the card along the centre lines. It helps if you score along the lines with the ruler first.

3 Paint one side of the card. Leave to dry, then paint the other side in a different colour. Leave to dry while you make the finger-holders.

4 Draw four small rectangles on thin card and cut out. Fold around into tubes to fit your middle finger and thumb, and glue together.

5 Decorate one side of the thick painted card. Draw around the pastry-cutters with a black felt-tipped pen to make outline shapes.

6 Reinforce the centre where the castanets bend with coloured sticky tape. This will make them last longer.

7 Glue the finger-holders onto the decorated side of the card. Place them about 1 cm (½ in) each side of the bend. Leave to dry.

8 Glue a pastry-cutter to the inside ends of each castanet. Use plenty of glue and let it dry properly.

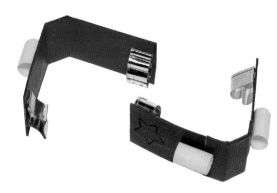

Dustbin Drum

Drums are very old instruments. They are used for the rhythm in dance music and they help soldiers to keep in step when they march. Drums were also once used to send signals because you can hear them so far away. You can play your drum with bare hands or with beaters, like Jessica and Alice.

Making music

Do not hit the drum too hard. You will get the best sound if you hit it close to the edge. If you hit different parts of the drumskin, you will get different sounds. Try playing it with a pair of chopsticks or your hands.

! A grown-up should cut the cork in half with a craft knife and push the skewer into the corks, to make the beaters. Children may need help with scissors.

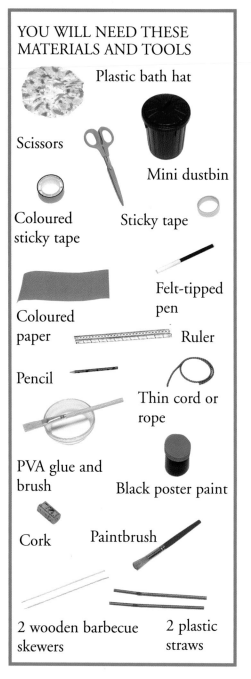

YOU WILL NEED THESE MATERIALS AND TOOLS

Plastic bath hat

Scissors

Mini dustbin

Coloured sticky tape

Sticky tape

Coloured paper

Felt-tipped pen

Ruler

Pencil

Thin cord or rope

PVA glue and brush

Black poster paint

Cork

Paintbrush

2 wooden barbecue skewers

2 plastic straws

The finished drum looks very smart.

1 Cut the elastic out of the bath hat. Draw around a plate which is 5 cm (2 in) bigger all around than the top of the dustbin. Cut the circle out.

2 Decorate the dustbin with stripes of coloured sticky tape.

3 Stretch the plastic circle tightly over the open end of the dustbin. Stick in place with several small tabs of sticky tape.

4 Make sure the plastic drumskin is really tight, then tape right around the edge to hold it in place.

5 Cut a strip of coloured paper to fit around the dustbin top. Make small cuts on both sides for a fringe.

6 Glue the fringe around the top of the dustbin.

7 Tie the cord or rope around the centre of the fringe.

8 Ask a grown-up to cut the cork in half across the middle. Paint the corks black. Push the skewers through the straws, then ask a grown-up to push them into the corks.

Deep Box Bass

Bass instruments play the very lowest notes. This is because they are so large. The large box and the large hole mean there is plenty of space for the air to vibrate and make a deep, booming sound. Nicholas is plucking his box bass with his fingers, like a double-bass player in a jazz band.

Your box bass is all ready for a jazz session!

Making music

Hold the elastic with one hand and twang it with the other. You can change the sound by pressing the elastic in different places. Thick elastic makes a lower sound than thin elastic.

! A grown-up should cut the cork in half with a craft knife. Children may need help with scissors.

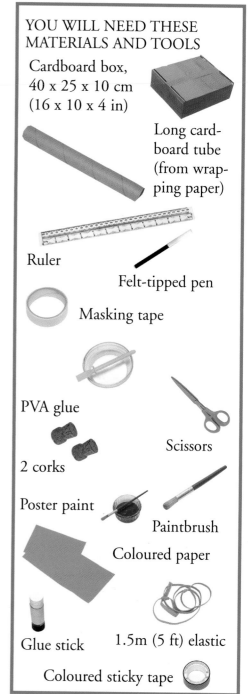

YOU WILL NEED THESE MATERIALS AND TOOLS

Cardboard box, 40 x 25 x 10 cm (16 x 10 x 4 in)

Long cardboard tube (from wrapping paper)

Ruler

Felt-tipped pen

Masking tape

PVA glue

Scissors

2 corks

Poster paint

Paintbrush

Coloured paper

Glue stick

1.5m (5 ft) elastic

Coloured sticky tape

1 Draw around the cardboard tube to make a circle on the centre of the box top. Then draw around the roll of masking tape to make a larger circle on the box front. Position it as shown.

2 Carefully cut out both circles. Pierce the circle with the scissors, and make small cuts out towards the edge of the circle. Then cut around the edge of the circle.

3 Push the tube through the small hole. Glue and tape the tube in place. Ask a grown-up to cut a cork in half. Glue and tape one half as shown and the other below the large hole.

4 Paint the box and the tube, and leave to dry.

5 Draw musical notes on the coloured paper. Draw around a cork to make the circle shapes.

6 Cut out the notes and glue them onto the front of the box.

7 Ask a grown-up to cut an 8 cm (3 in) slit in the front of the tube. Tie the elastic around the bottom. Tie a double knot in the other end.

8 Decorate the box with tape. Stretch the elastic down the back of the box and back up the front. Slip the knot into the slit in the tube.

Singing Kazoo

This is a very unusual instrument. You sing through it and it makes your voice sound very strange. Indian musicians play a kind of kazoo which they hold against their throats when they sing. Lorenzo has covered his kazoo with stencils. This is a very easy and quick way to decorate things.

Making music

Sing through the hole in the middle of the kazoo. You can play any tune you like. Experiment with a smaller tube from a toilet roll, and see if it sounds different.

! A grown-up should make the hole in the cardboard tube and sticky tape. Children may need help with scissors.

YOU WILL NEED THESE MATERIALS AND TOOLS

Cardboard tube (from kitchen paper or foil)

Scissors

Paintbrushes

Poster paint, in white and 2 colours

Paper doily

Masking tape

Greaseproof paper

Felt-tipped pen

PVA glue and brush

40 cm (16 in) paper ribbon

Coloured sticky tape

Stencils are a good way to decorate any of the instruments.

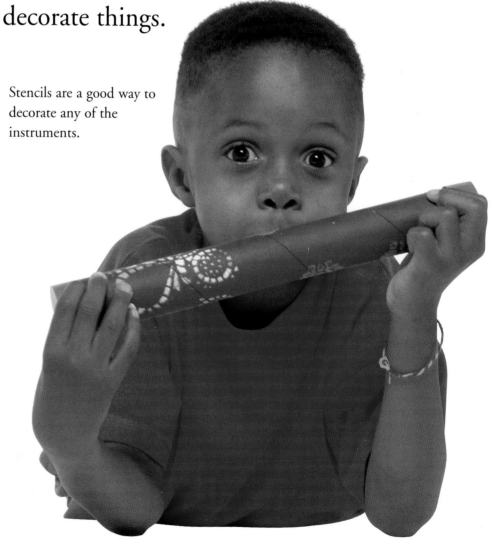

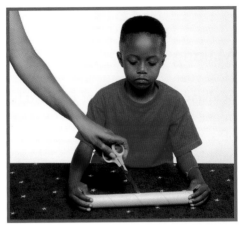

1 Ask a grown-up to make a small hole
in the centre of the cardboard tube.

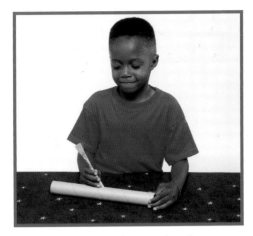

2 Use the end of a paintbrush to
smooth the edges of the hole.

3 Paint the cardboard tube. Leave
the paint to dry.

4 Cut flower shapes from the paper
doily and use them as stencils.
Stick them onto the tube with masking
tape and paint over them. Leave the
paint to dry, then remove the stencils.

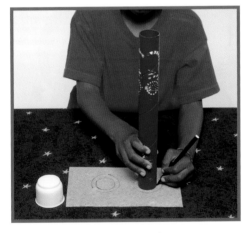

5 Draw two circles on the greaseproof paper. Draw around a cup or
any round object that is slightly larger
than the end of the tube. Now draw
around the end of the tube to make a
smaller circle inside each larger one.

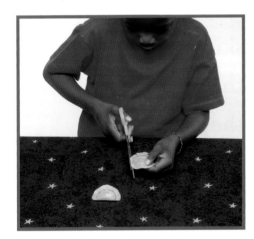

6 Cut out the large circles. Make
small cuts between the large and
small circles. This will give each circle a
frill around the edge. Brush glue onto
the frills.

7 Stretch the greaseproof paper
circles tightly across the ends of
the cardboard tube. Press the frills
around the sides of the tube.

8 Glue ribbon around the ends of the
tube. Stick a piece of coloured
sticky tape over the hole. Ask a grown-
up to pierce through the tape.

Shoebox Guitar

The guitar is probably the most popular instrument of all. It is easy to carry and you can play many different kinds of music on it. Jessica is plucking the elastic string on her guitar, just like a pop star. Electric guitars don't have boxes full of air like this one, so they need electricity to make them sound loud.

Making music
Pluck the elastic string with one hand. With your other hand, press the elastic against the cardboard tube. If you press, in different places, you can change the note. Try strumming the string with a coin instead of plucking it.

! Children may need help cutting out the circles. See the Introduction for an easy way of doing this.

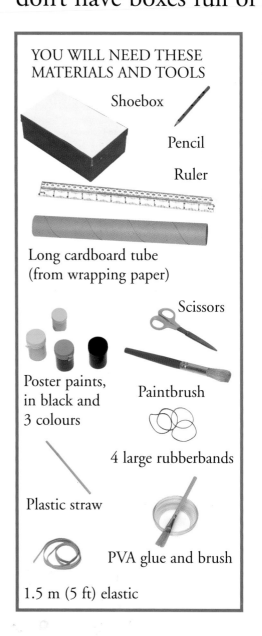

YOU WILL NEED THESE MATERIALS AND TOOLS

Shoebox

Pencil

Ruler

Long cardboard tube (from wrapping paper)

Scissors

Poster paints, in black and 3 colours

Paintbrush

4 large rubberbands

Plastic straw

PVA glue and brush

1.5 m (5 ft) elastic

A guitar is a large box full of air. The air vibrates and makes the sound, which escapes through the hole.

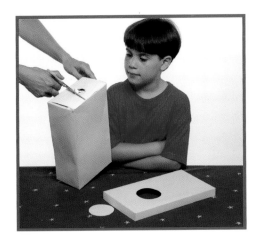

1 Draw a 10 cm (4 in) circle on the box lid. Draw around the tube on one end of the box base. Ask a grown-up to cut out the circles.

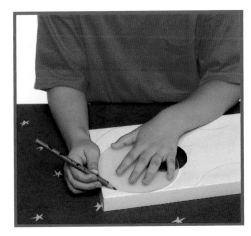

2 Draw a guitar shape on the lid of the box. Use a circular shape as a guide, or use a pair of compasses, if you like.

3 Outline the guitar shape in black paint. Fill in with coloured paint, then paint the rest of the box another colour. Paint the tube.

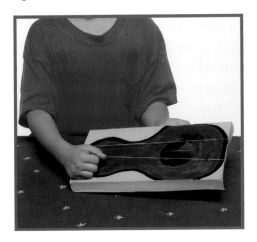

4 Stretch two rubberbands across the lid. Position them as shown, just on the edge of the hole.

5 Put the lid on the box. Hold it in place with two more rubberbands. Cut the straw in half. Slide the two pieces under the rubberbands at each end of the guitar. Glue in place.

6 Cut a slit about 8 cm (3 in) long at one end of the tube. Tie a knot in one end of the elastic. Make a loop in the other end and slide it over the end of the tube.

7 Push the tube into the hole in the box. Stretch the elastic around the back of the box and up around the front. Slip the knot into the slit in the tube.

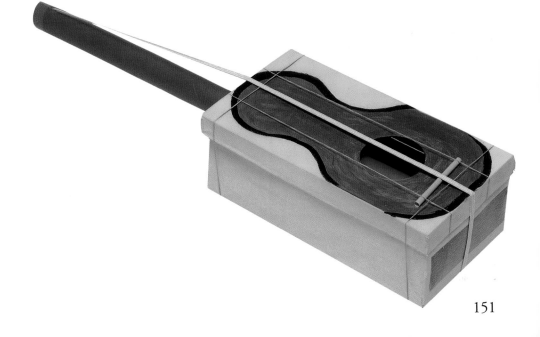

151

Caxixi Rattle

The name of this rattle is pronounced "casheeshee". It comes from Latin America. You can fill it with anything that will make a good sound – try rice or beans, or sand. Alice has made a face for her rattle with scraps of paper and stickers. She has also given it a wonderful fringe.

⚠️ A grown-up should puncture the bottle and children may need help with scissors.

Shake your caxixi rattle in time to your favourite music.

Making music

Make two caxixi rattles and shake them together. Practise until you can keep in time to the rhythm of the music. Fill the bottles with different things to make different sounds.

YOU WILL NEED THESE MATERIALS AND TOOLS

Felt-tipped pens

Small plastic bottle

Scissors

Funnel

Sticky tape

Poster paint

Lentils or rice

PVA glue and brush

Paintbrush

2 sheets of paper, in different colours

Ruler

Pencil

Coloured stickers

Coloured sticky tape

1 Wash and dry the bottle. Draw a line around the bottle about one-third from the top. Draw another line the same distance from the bottom.

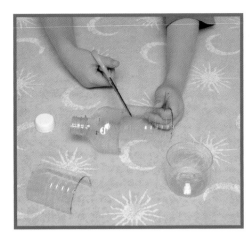

2 Ask a grown-up to puncture the bottle with the point of the scissors. Then cut along both the lines you have marked.

3 Stick the top and bottom pieces of the bottle together with sticky tape to make a shorter bottle shape. Pour the lentils or rice into the bottle.

4 Mix the paint with glue and a little water and paint the top half of the bottle. Leave to dry.

5 Cut a strip from each of the coloured sheets of paper, long enough to wrap around the bottle.

6 To make a fringe, fold the strips over and make plenty of small cuts halfway across the strips of paper.

7 Glue the fringe around the bottle. Hold it in place with coloured tape. Decorate your caxixi with a funny face using the coloured stickers, the paper and the felt-tipped pen.

This is a different caxixi shape made from a drinks can and decorated with star stickers and coloured sticky tape.

153

Saucepan Lid Cymbals

Saucepan lids make terrific cymbals. You can hit one with a beater, or clash them together as Benjamin is doing. Be careful not to bang them directly together – to do a proper cymbal clash, you move one cymbal up and one down. Real cymbals can turn inside-out if you hit them directly together! Cymbals are often played with drums in a drum kit.

Making music

Cymbals are often played very loudly, but they can also make a lovely, quiet sound. You can also hold a cymbal by its handle, or hang is from a piece of string, and strike it with one of your homemade beaters.

! A grown-up should cut the cork in half using a craft knife. Children will need help pushing the skewer into the cork.

YOU WILL NEED THESE MATERIALS AND TOOLS

2 matching metal saucepan lids

Coloured stickers

Ribbon

Scissors

Narrow and wide coloured sticky tape

Large bottle-washer

Wooden barbecue skewer

Pan scourer

Cork

If you want to decorate your saucepan lid cymbals, check with a grown-up first to make sure they don't mind.

1 Decorate the saucepan lids with coloured stickers. Arrange them in a circle, following the shape of the lid. Decorate the ribbon with stickers.

2 Decorate the handles with several strips of ribbon. Loop the strips around the handle and stick together with narrow coloured sticky tape.

3 Cover the rest of the handles with wide coloured sticky tape. Wind the narrow tape around the handle to make stripes.

4 Now make the first stick. Decorate the handle of the bottle-washer with coloured stickers and sticky tape.

5 Make the second stick. Push the wooden skewer through the middle of the pan scourer. Ask a grown-up to cut the cork in half. Push the sharp end of the skewer into one piece of cork.

6 Wind coloured sticky tape around the cork and the skewer where it comes out below the pan scourer. This will stop the pan scourer from slipping down the handle.

The two beaters make different sounds.

Snakey Maracas

Maracas are played by shaking them in time to the music. The rice inside rattles around to make the sound. Maracas are very popular in Africa and Latin America, where they are often made out of gourds. Nicholas has made his maracas out of papier mâché. This is wet newspaper mixed with glue. When it is dry, it sets hard so that you can paint it.

! Children may need help blowing up and tying the balloons, and with cutting the holes in the papier mâché.

When you play your maracas, the snakes will wriggle about and frighten everyone.

Making music
Shake both maracas together in time to the music. You can also play one maraca on its own. Hold it in one hand and roll it against the palm of your other hand.

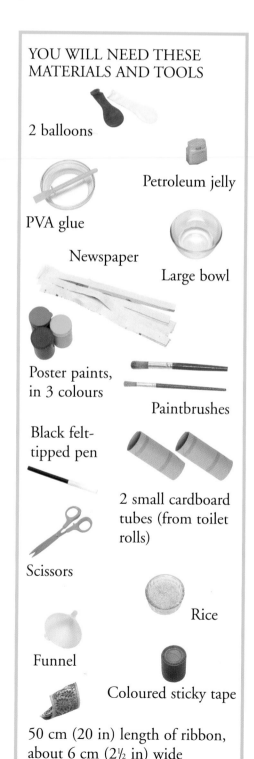

YOU WILL NEED THESE MATERIALS AND TOOLS

2 balloons

Petroleum jelly

PVA glue

Newspaper

Large bowl

Poster paints, in 3 colours

Paintbrushes

Black felt-tipped pen

2 small cardboard tubes (from toilet rolls)

Scissors

Rice

Funnel

Coloured sticky tape

50 cm (20 in) length of ribbon, about 6 cm (2½ in) wide

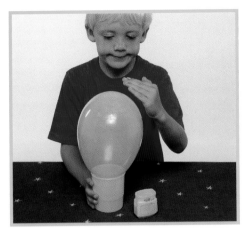

1 Blow up and tie the balloons. Cover them with petroleum jelly. Support the balloons in jars or mugs, otherwise they will bounce about.

2 Tear the newspaper into strips and squares. Soak them in glue. Cover the balloons with the strips. Leave to dry, then cover them with the squares.

3 Wait for the second layer to dry, then paint the balloons. Leave the paint to dry.

4 Now paint the cardboard tubes, using a different colour. Leave the paint to dry.

5 Draw around one of the cardboard tubes on the end of each balloon and cut out the circles.

6 Spread glue onto one end of each cardboard tube. Push them into the holes in the balloons for handles.

7 Pour the rice into the balloons through the handles. Seal the end of each handle with coloured sticky tape. Spread glue onto the handles, then cover them with ribbon.

8 Paint squiggly snakes to decorate the maracas. Use the black felt-tipped pen to draw the snakes' eyes and their forked tongues.

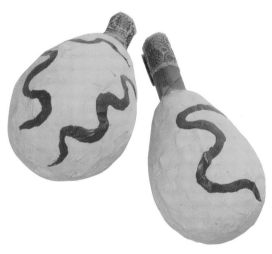

Bottle Xylophone

Bottles make wonderful musical instruments. To get different notes, you add more water. Play the xylophone with different sticks to make different sounds. You can also blow across the top of the bottles. Gabriella has put coloured water in her xylophone bottles. This looks pretty and it also helps her remember the different notes.

⚠️ A grown-up should push the skewer into the cork. Never leave the coloured water in the bottles in case someone is tempted to try a taste. The water is NOT drinkable.

The different sticks make different sounds. What other sticks could you use?

Making music

See if you can play a simple tune like "Three Blind Mice". Add a little water to each bottle or pour some out until you get the notes right.

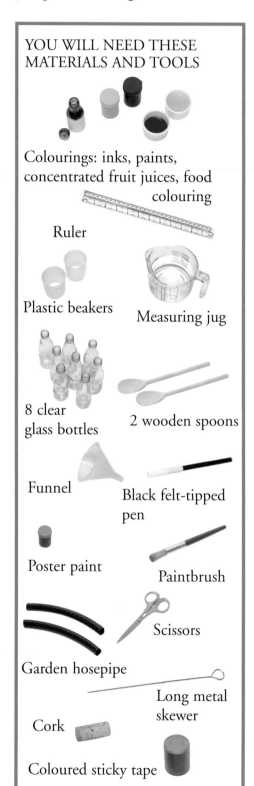

YOU WILL NEED THESE MATERIALS AND TOOLS

Colourings: inks, paints, concentrated fruit juices, food colouring

Ruler

Plastic beakers

Measuring jug

8 clear glass bottles

2 wooden spoons

Funnel

Black felt-tipped pen

Poster paint

Paintbrush

Garden hosepipe

Scissors

Cork

Long metal skewer

Coloured sticky tape

1 Mix seven different colours with water. Use inks, paints, concentrated fruit juices or food colouring.

2 Hit one of the glass bottles with a wooden spoon and listen to the sound it makes.

3 Mark 2 cm (¾ in) from the bottom of the bottle. Use a felt-tipped pen.

4 Pour water into the bottle up to the mark. This is much easier if you use a funnel. Hit the bottle again – this time the sound will be lower.

5 Pour a different coloured water into each bottle. Raise the level of the water by 2 cm (¾ in) each time. The bottle with the most water will give the lowest note.

6 Now try blowing across the top of each bottle. This time the bottle with the most water will give the highest note!

7 Paint the round ends of two wooden spoons. Cover the handles with hosepipe.

8 Make a different stick. Ask a grown-up to cut the cork in half and push in the skewer. Cover the cork with sticky tape.

Bugle Blow

The first bugles were used to send signals in battle or out hunting. Today bugles are used in the army, to wake everyone up in the morning! The soldier's bugle is a brass instrument but Claudius's bugle is made from a garden hosepipe. To get a good sound from this kind of instrument, you need a mouthpiece.

You will need plenty of puff to play your bugle.

Making music
Rest the rim of the mouthpiece on your lips and take a deep breath. Buzz your lips into the mouthpiece. To play higher notes, blow faster.

! Children may need help cutting and positioning the hosepipe.

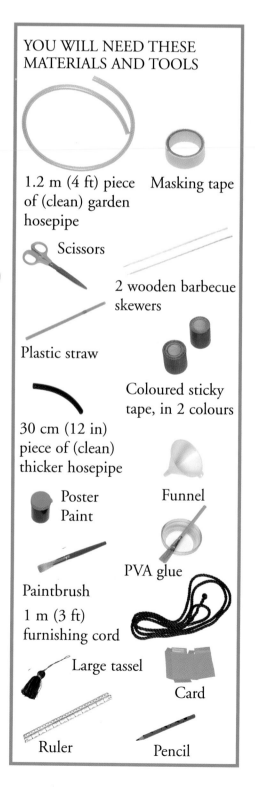

YOU WILL NEED THESE MATERIALS AND TOOLS

1.2 m (4 ft) piece of (clean) garden hosepipe   Masking tape

Scissors

2 wooden barbecue skewers

Plastic straw

Coloured sticky tape, in 2 colours

30 cm (12 in) piece of (clean) thicker hosepipe

Poster Paint   Funnel

PVA glue

Paintbrush

1 m (3 ft) furnishing cord

Large tassel   Card

Ruler   Pencil

160

1 Bend the thin hosepipe into a circle so that the ends overlap as shown. Bind the circle together with two pieces of masking tape 8 cm (3 in) apart.

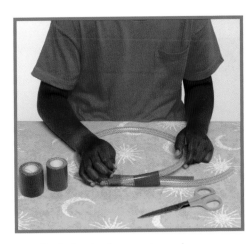

2 Push both skewers into the straw. Place the straw behind the join in the hosepipe and tape them together in three places.

3 Cut a piece of thick hosepipe about 15 cm (6 in) long. Slide it onto one end of the hosepipe. Cut a shorter length and slide it onto the other end.

4 Mix the poster paint with the same amount of glue and a little water, and then paint the funnel. Push the funnel into the longer piece of thick hosepipe.

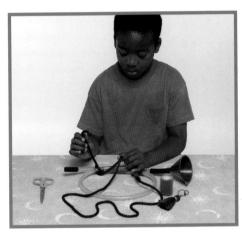

5 Tie the cord onto the bugle so that you can carry it across your chest. Fasten the tassel to the bugle.

6 Measure a square about 13 x 13 cm (5 x 5 in) on the card and cut out.

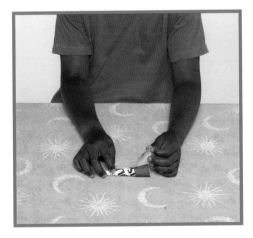

7 Roll the square into a cone shape and trim. Tape the cone together and tape over the sharp card edges.

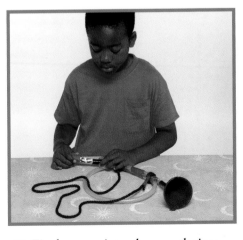

8 Fit the cone into the mouthpiece end of the bugle.

161

Flowerpot Chimes

You do not have to play these wind chimes yourself – if you hang them up the wind will play them for you. The best place to hang them is from a door frame or window frame. Ilaira likes to play her chimes herself, using wooden spoons. The flowerpots are very heavy, so you need a strong coathanger.

Making music
Hit the flowerpots gently with the spoons. Does the small flowerpot sound different to the large one?

!A grown-up should make the holes in the corks and cut them in half with a craft knife. Children may need help with scissors.

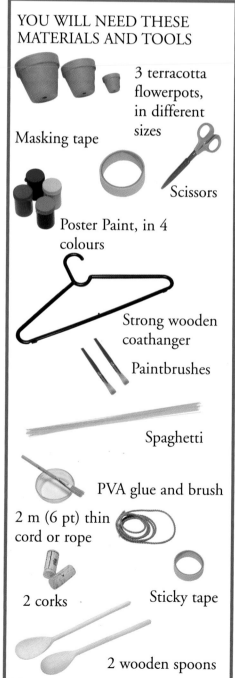

YOU WILL NEED THESE
MATERIALS AND TOOLS

3 terracotta flowerpots, in different sizes

Masking tape

Scissors

Poster Paint, in 4 colours

Strong wooden coathanger

Paintbrushes

Spaghetti

PVA glue and brush

2 m (6 pt) thin cord or rope

2 corks

Sticky tape

2 wooden spoons

The finished flowerpot chimes, ready to play a tune. Ilaira has painted her spoons bright green.

162

1 Use the masking tape to make four triangle shapes on each pot. Paint above the tape in different colours. Leave to dry, then pull off the tape.

2 Tape along the edge of the painted area. Then paint below the tape in another colour. Leave to dry and remove the tape.

3 Decorate the coathanger. Use as many colours as possible to make it really bright. Paint the wooden spoons too, if you like.

4 Ask a grown-up to cook some spaghetti. Keep it soft in warm water until you glue it onto the pots. Hold the spaghetti in place with masking tape until the glue is dry.

5 Mix the paints together to make brown and paint the spaghetti. Try not to paint the pots underneath. Leave to dry.

6 Cut the cord into three pieces. Ask a grown-up to make a hole in the corks and cut them in half. Thread a cork on each cord and tie a knot in one end.

7 Thread the other end of the cord through the hole in the bottom of the flowerpot.

8 Tie each piece of cord to the coathanger. Tie a good knot, then bind the cord with sticky tape.

I Can Have a Party!

Christmas Tree Hat

Nicholas has made a hat especially to celebrate Christmas. It shows the star of Bethlehem, which sits on the top of Christmas trees. He will definitely be the star of the party. You can make other hats, too, such as a sunshine hat or a flower hat for a summer party. Make the hat in the same way but with a big sun or flower instead of a star.

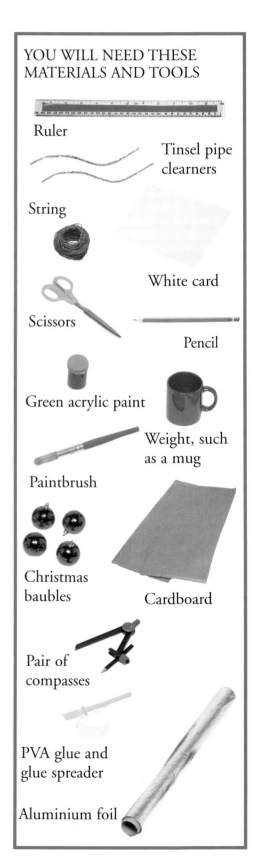

YOU WILL NEED THESE MATERIALS AND TOOLS

Ruler

Tinsel pipe clearners

String

White card

Scissors

Pencil

Green acrylic paint

Weight, such as a mug

Paintbrush

Christmas baubles

Cardboard

Pair of compasses

PVA glue and glue spreader

Aluminium foil

1 Measure your head with the piece of string, then add 8 cm onto the length of the string.

2 Cut a piece of white card the same length as the string. Draw a dotted line down the centre. Draw a Christmas tree shape with tabs top and sides.

3 Cut out the tree shape with the tabs at the top and sides. Paint it green and leave it to dry.

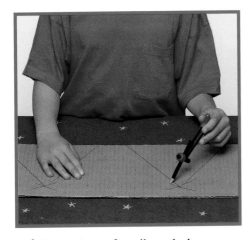

4 On a piece of cardboard, draw and cut out two triangles with 18 cm sides. Draw the bottom of the triangle first, then use the compasses to mark the top point.

5 Stick the two triangles together to make a star with six points. Glue aluminium foil onto the star and leave it to dry.

6 Glue the tab at the top of the tree to the back of the star. Leave it to dry under a weight, so the two pieces bond strongly together. Ask a grown-up to trim the tabs to fit.

7 Glue or tape the side tabs together, so the hat fits your head. Leave to dry. Tape tinsel around the hat.

8 Use tinsel pipe cleaners to tie Christmas baubles around the hat.

Treasure Chest

Aimee has made a treasure chest and she has filled it with lots of consolation prizes, so that each of her guests leaves the party with a going-away present. She has wrapped all the presents in gold paper, so that they look like treasure, and added bags of chocolate coins. The presents don't need to be big or expensive, just fun. She is going to hide her treasure trove until the end of the party, then everyone will play "hunt the treasure chest". The winner gets the first pick of the prizes.

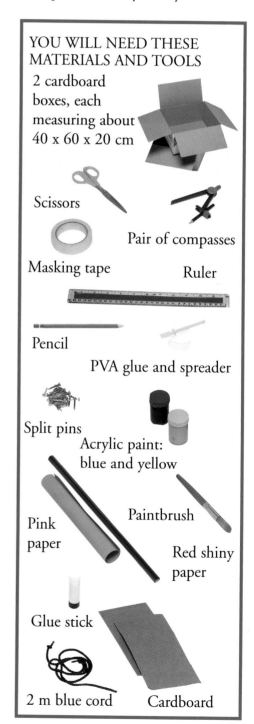

Safety tip
When making holes with a pair of scissors, always make sure the blades are closed together and that you point the tip of them away from you.

YOU WILL NEED THESE MATERIALS AND TOOLS
2 cardboard boxes, each measuring about 40 x 60 x 20 cm

Scissors

Pair of compasses

Masking tape

Ruler

Pencil

PVA glue and spreader

Split pins

Acrylic paint: blue and yellow

Pink paper

Paintbrush

Red shiny paper

Glue stick

2 m blue cord

Cardboard

1 Cut three of the flaps off one of the boxes, leaving one of the long flaps. This will be used later for the lid.

2 Cut up the second box, leaving the base, one long and two short sides. Draw a semicircle on each short side.

3 Use the compass to draw the semicircles, as shown in the picture for Step 2. Cut them out.

4 Fold up the semicircles to make the sides of the lid. Place the long side of the box in the middle and hold in place with masking tape.

5 Cut a 60 cm square of cardboard. Ask a grown-up to score the cardboard to help it bend. Glue it to the sides and secure with masking tape.

6 Cut the flap on the first box to make two hinges. Glue the lid onto the hinges and leave to dry. Stud with split pins, putting glue under each pin.

7 Paint the outside of the chest with blue acrylic paint. With the glue stick, stick on yellow stripes to create a barrel effect. Add a keyhole and pink skulls and crossbones.

8 Line the chest with paper. Pierce two holes in either side of the box base. Thread cord into each and knot, then glue onto the lid. Hold in place with masking tape until dry.

Palm Trees

Treasure Island parties are great for having adventures. You can dress up as pirates and sailors. Nicholas is making some palm trees to put on the table with all the party food. An adult could help you to make larger palm trees, to stick in the garden flower beds. All you need to do is make them with larger sheets of paper or stick several sheets of paper together.

Where to put it
Put your palm trees in places where they won't easily get knocked over!

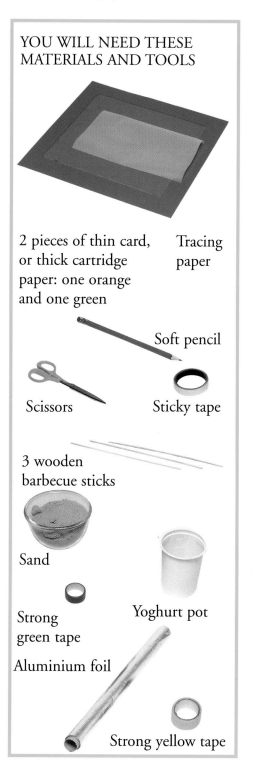

YOU WILL NEED THESE MATERIALS AND TOOLS

2 pieces of thin card, or thick cartridge paper: one orange and one green

Tracing paper

Soft pencil

Scissors

Sticky tape

3 wooden barbecue sticks

Sand

Yoghurt pot

Strong green tape

Aluminium foil

Strong yellow tape

1 Draw a leaf 40 cm long and 20 cm wide on green card. Use the guide to help you. Fold the leaf in half and cut it out. Make three for each tree.

2 Roll the orange card into a long tube. Hold the tube firmly, so that it doesn't uncurl, and cut a fringe into the top edge of the roll.

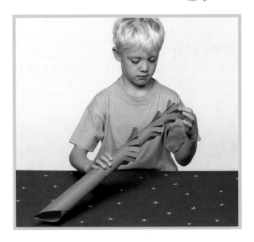

3 Still holding the tube firmly, gently pull out the inside edge of the card. Pull it right out to make the trunk of your tree.

4 Use sticky tape to hold the trunk together at the base. Trim the base, so that the trunk can stand up straight.

5 Tape a barbecue stick down the middle of each palm leaf with green tape.

6 Snip two slits on opposite sides of the trunk, just big enough to take the stalk of the leaf. Make the slits 10 cm from the top of the trunk.

7 Slide a palm leaf into each slit. Push the third leaf into the top of the trunk and tape it in place.

8 Cover the yoghurt pot with aluminium foil. Stick stripes on it with yellow tape. Fill the pot with sand and push the palm tree into it.

Arty Party Wall

Making a fun wall is always a huge success at parties. Party goers can draw on it, and leave messages or their names. Here Christopher has drawn a picture of the sea, but you can choose any theme. Leave lots of crayons and pencils in jars next to the wall. You'll be left with a masterpiece.

Material brainwave
If you can't get hold of a large roll of coloured paper, buy some lining paper or simple patterned wallpaper from a decorating shop.

YOU WILL NEED THESE
MATERIALS AND TOOLS

Several sheets of coloured paper

Scissors

Pencils in different colours

Glue stick

I large roll of paper, approximately 1 m square

Drawing pins

Ballons

Strong black tape

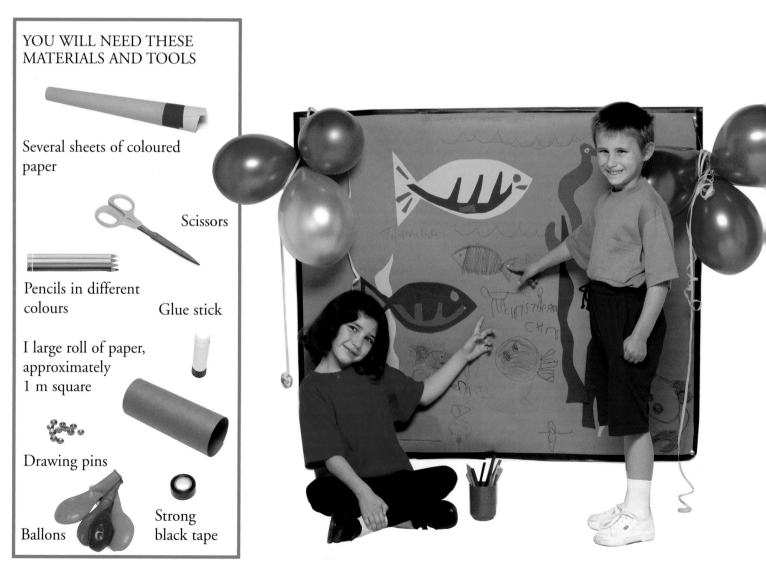

1 Cut out long wiggly strips of green paper to make seaweed.

2 Draw the outlines of some fish onto coloured paper, using light pencils on dark paper. The fish should be quite large. Cut them out neatly.

3 Cut out eyes and patterns in coloured paper and stick them onto your fish with a glue stick.

4 Pin or tape your large sheet of paper to the wall. Decorate the corners with balloons. Ask a grown-up to help if you are using drawing pins.

5 Stick on your cut-out fish and seaweed. Arrange them so that they look nice, but leave room for other drawings too.

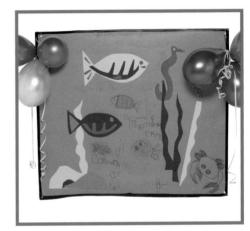

6 At your party, draw on lots of other creatures with your friends. You could write messages and add streamers to the decorations too.

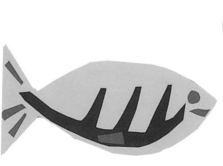

Gone Fishing

Houw is making a fishing game. Each player has to hook up as many floating fish as possible when the music is on. The player who catches the most fish wins. This game is best played in the garden or kitchen, as it's easy to splash lots of water around.

Houw has used washing-up bowls to make his fish ponds, but paddling pools are great as well.

Material note

The number of rods and bottles will depend on how many friends want to play. Make sure there are about three fish bottles per player.

YOU WILL NEED THESE MATERIALS AND TOOLS

10–20 small plastic drinks bottles with screw tops

Paintbrush

Acrylic paint

PVA glue and glue spreader

String

10–12 curtain rings

5 bamboo sticks

Scissors

Blue food colouring

Strong coloured tape

5 plastic-coated screw-in cup hooks

Tissue paper

2 or 3 washing-up bowls

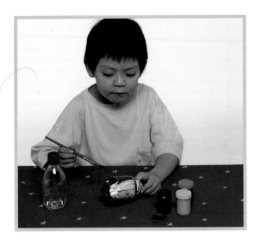

1 Wash the drinks bottles and soak off the labels. Leave to dry, then screw the lids back on. Paint fish shapes onto the bottles. Mix glue into your paint so that it sticks to the plastic.

2 Cut string into lengths of 45 cm. Tie the end of each piece of string onto the hook in a curtain ring. Do this with as many curtain rings as there are bottles.

3 Tie the string onto the bottles with a double knot, so that the curtain ring dangles a bit.

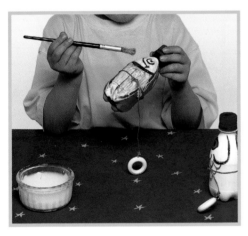

4 To make the paint waterproof, mix a varnish of three parts glue to one part water. Apply two coats to the painted fish bottles. Leave the glue to dry between coats.

5 To make the fishing rods, decorate the bamboo sticks with bands of coloured tape.

6 Screw a cup hook firmly into the end of each rod.

7 Wrap tissue around the bowls. Add food colouring to the water.

Marzipan Dinosaur Cake

Marzipan is the delicious almond decoration you find on the top of birthday cakes. You can buy marzipan from any supermarket and it's easy to colour it with food dye. Decorate a ready-made cake for yourself or for someone in your family or a friend. Before you roll the marzipan, wash your hands.

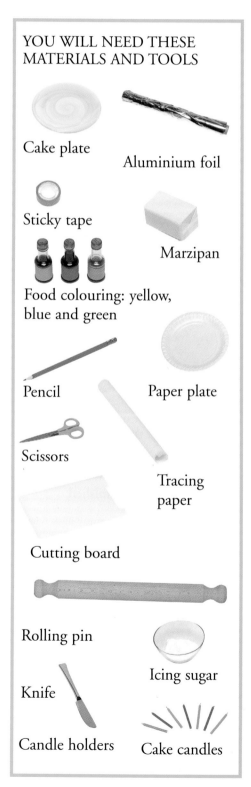

YOU WILL NEED THESE MATERIALS AND TOOLS

Cake plate

Aluminium foil

Sticky tape

Marzipan

Food colouring: yellow, blue and green

Pencil

Paper plate

Scissors

Tracing paper

Cutting board

Rolling pin

Icing sugar

Knife

Candle holders

Cake candles

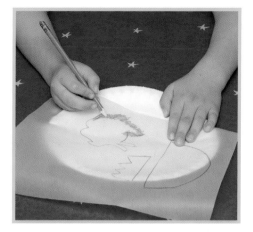

1 Cover the plate with aluminium foil and use a little sticky tape on the back to hold it.

2 Add food colouring to the marzipan, only a couple of drops at a time. Knead it in thoroughly.

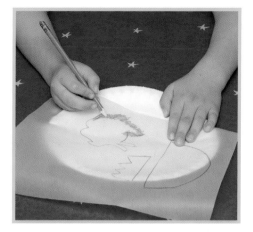

3 Trace the dinosaur template and transfer it onto the paper plate, using a soft pencil.

4 Cut out the dinosaur and the other shapes.

5 Roll out the marzipan until it is 5–10 mm thick. Sprinkle a little icing sugar onto the rolling pin and surface to stop the marzipan sticking.

6 Ask a grown-up to cut out the marzipan with a knife, using your card cut-outs as a guide.

7 Put the cake onto the plate covered in aluminium foil and carefully lay the marzipan on the cake. You can help the shapes stay in place by dabbing a bit of water underneath.

8 Push the candles into the holders, then decorate the cake with them. Light the candles and it's time to sing "Happy Birthday"!

Funny Faces Fairy Cakes

These are cakes you can either decorate before your guests arrive, or make into a game at the party. Lay out all the materials and see which guest can make the silliest face or the most imaginative object out of the cakes. Iza and Gaby have made funny faces with mad hair.

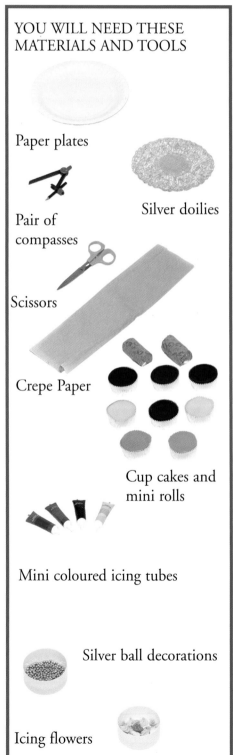

YOU WILL NEED THESE MATERIALS AND TOOLS

Paper plates

Silver doilies

Pair of compasses

Scissors

Crepe Paper

Cup cakes and mini rolls

Mini coloured icing tubes

Silver ball decorations

Icing flowers

1 Put a silver doily on a paper plate. Using compasses, draw a slightly smaller circle on crepe paper and cut it out. Place it on top of the doily.

2 Place a cup cake and a mini roll on the plate. These will make the head and body.

3 Squeezing the mini icing tubes gently, pipe on the mouth, eyes and nose, using different colours.

4 Put silver balls on the eyes to make them sparkle.

5 To make the jacket, ice on stripes and buttons. Add icing flower decorations and silver balls.

6 Add some curly hair with a different colour of icing.

7 Add arms, hands and a skirt by piping coloured icing straight onto the pink paper. Add some icing flowers for the feet and your work of art is ready to eat!

I Can Make Magic

Introduction

So, you want to be a magician? Good! Because magic is fun. Actually, it is *great* fun. Making the tricks is fun, doing the tricks is fun and, most of all, entertaining people with magic is fun.

Some people, and books, say magic is very hard to do because it needs hour after hour, year after year, of never-ending practice. Well, in this chapter you will find lots of tricks that you will be able to do easily with only a little practice. And once you've learnt how to do all the projects shown here, you might go on to learn the more complicated secrets of magic.

Making Things For Your Magic

The Wand

In order to practise magic, you need a few essential props. The most important of these is your wand. You can make one yourself. All you need is a 30 cm length of round wood,

called dowel, some masking tape and black and white poster paints. Wrap masking tape around each end of the dowel and paint the wood in-between black. When the paint is dry,

remove the tape and paint the ends white. Hey presto! The stick has magically become a wand, ready for you to do some brilliant tricks with.

The Magic Box

An essential prop is a beautifully coloured magic box. This box means you will be able to produce many things you need for your show, out of a box that seems to be empty!

1 First tape over the sharp edges of an empty 850 g baked bean tin. Then glue a rectangle of red card together at the edges, to make a tube wider and taller than the tin. For the outer box, join four identical pieces of stiff card together with masking tape. Ask a grown-up to help you cut out some holes in one piece for the front of the box.

2 Here Lucy has decorated the box to look like an old-fashioned radio. Now paint half of the bean tin and the inside of the box with black poster paint. When the paint is dry, fill the tin with magical things.

3 Put the bean tin, filled with silk handkerchiefs, cards, a small pink rabbit and a plastic fried egg, inside the box. Can you see it? No? That is because you place it in the box with its black side facing the holes in the front, so when you lift out the red tube the box appears empty. After putting the red tube back over the bean tin, you can lift up the radio box, because it has no bottom, to show that it is empty as well.

4 This "illusion" means that Lucy can produce the hankies, cards and rabbit from an "empty" box. She can turn the tin around when it is inside the tube and lift it out, with the egg, to add a funny finish to her trick. Now, once she has put the tin and egg away, she can again show her audience that the tube and box are both empty. This time, as there is nothing left to hide, she can hold the tube and box up together.

193

The Hat

Every self-respecting magician has a top hat, and it is needed for many of the tricks in this book.

1 Ask a friend to measure around your head. Add 2 cm to the figure and cut a piece of stiff black paper to this length, and about 15 cm wide. Roll the paper into a tube and glue the edges together.

2 For the top of the hat, place the tube upright on a sheet of black paper and draw round it with a white crayon. Draw a second circle about 1 cm wider around the first circle and cut out the outer line. Cut small "V"s around the whole shape between the outer and inner circles. Glue the tabs downwards inside the top of the tube. To make the brim, draw round the shape of your hat onto more black paper. Draw a second circle 1 cm smaller than your tube and a third circle 5 cm larger. Cut out along these last two lines. Cut tabs again and glue them into the bottom of your hat.

3 A secret flap fixed inside your magician's top hat is perfect for hiding things. Cut out a round piece of stiff black paper to fit snugly down into the hat. Tape a flap onto the middle of it with masking tape. Paint the tape black and cut the flap into a semicircle so that it can be held against either side of the hat, with your fingers. If you briefly tip the opening of the hat towards the audience, anything hidden behind the flap will not be seen. They will just see blackness inside the hat and assume the hat is empty.

4 Add some ribbon to the hat to finish it off. Measure round the tube of your hat, and add 1 cm to this. Glue the ribbon round the hat just above the brim with a 1 cm overlap. A black or coloured bow tie will make you really look like a magician.

Performing

Performing magic is all about acting the part of the magician convincingly. When you are doing a trick you must try to believe that magic is really happening. If you believe it, so will your audience.

What to Say

What you say to your audience during your show is called your "patter". The most important thing is to be natural. Talk in your own way. Make up a story to go with the trick and add a few jokes if you would like to get a laugh.

Repeating Tricks

When you have done a good trick, people will ask to see it again. Don't be tempted to repeat it! Your audience might discover the secret of the trick the second time round.

Misdirection

This is the art of making your audience look where *you* want them to look. The audience will look where your eyes are looking or at your moving hands. If you are hiding a coin in your hand, don't look at that hand. Also, never say that a box or hat is "empty" or the audience will be suspicious. Quickly show them the inside and they will assume that it is empty.

Secrets

Always keep your magic secrets to yourself. Store your magic things out of sight, in a case or a closed box.

Appearance

Look smart and especially have clean hands and fingernails. Smile. Look happy. If you feel a little shy in front of an audience, try your tricks out in private first, and even in front of a mirror.

Mistakes

Sometimes things will go wrong (even the most famous magicians sometimes make mistakes!). Don't panic. If you can, correct things and carry on. If you can't, just smile and get the audience involved in another trick. Remember that your audience is there because they want to be entertained and they want you to do well. Practising your tricks in front of a mirror will help prevent the mistakes from happening.

Magic Secrets

Part of the skill of being a magician is keeping things to yourself. In order to show how to do things, we have taken photographs, but whenever you see the top hat symbol, this is a view that the audience should not see.

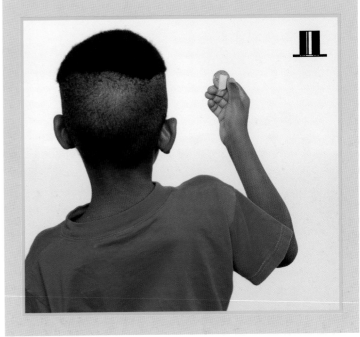

How Many Tricks?

Don't make your show too long. That way you will leave your audience wanting more and they will ask you for another show on another day. Plan a short show that has a beginning, a middle and an end. And don't forget – smile!

Magic Words

In magic there are many special words. Here are some useful ones for you to learn.

EFFECT What the audience sees.

GAG A joke or a funny story.

GIMMICK OR FAKE A secret part of the prop that the audience does not see.

ILLUSION When something *seems* to happen but doesn't.

LOAD The things held in a secret compartment.

PALMING Keeping something hidden in your hand.

PATTER Your talk that goes with the trick.

PRODUCTION Making something appear from nowhere.

PROPS The things you use for your tricks.

ROUTINE A series of tricks or moves.

SHUFFLE To mix up cards in your hands.

SILKS Silk handkerchiefs.

SLEEVING Hiding something up your sleeve to make it vanish or ready to appear in your hand later.

SLEIGHT OF HAND A clever movement of your hand to make magic.

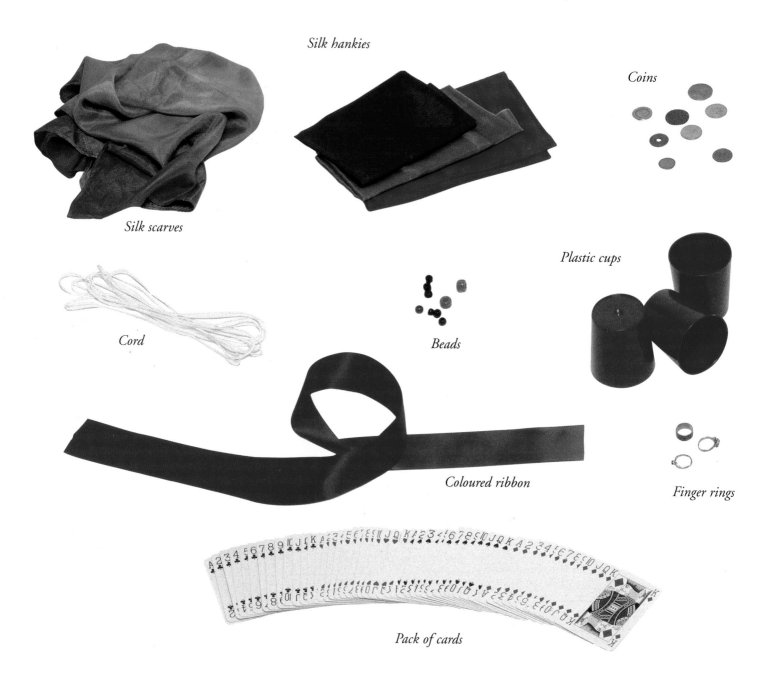

Silk hankies

Coins

Silk scarves

Cord

Beads

Plastic cups

Coloured ribbon

Finger rings

Pack of cards

STEAL To move something from its place secretly.

SWITCH To change one thing for another secretly.

TALK The sound that hidden objects might make – for example, rattle, click, etc.

TRANSPOSITION When something magically disappears from one place to reappear in another.

VANISH To make an object seem to disappear.

Materials

The materials that you will need are always listed. Gather them all together before you start. Work on a suitable surface. Wear an apron if you are painting or gluing, and tidy everything away afterwards. Allow time for paint and glue to dry before moving on to the next stage. Keep a collection of empty cartons, tubes and boxes, etc. Once they have been painted and decorated they are great for magic. Take great care when using scissors or other sharp instruments, and always ask a grown-up to help if you need to use a craft knife.

Black is a very useful colour in magic because a black object in black surroundings becomes almost invisible. So, if the instructions for a trick say to use black, then *do* use black. Finally, take your time and study the photographs and the text carefully. If a photograph shows someone doing a trick with their right hand and you prefer to use your left, don't worry. Just swap things over and do it your own way.

Chocolate money

'Joke' fried egg

Large envelopes

Soft rope

Rubber bands

Paper napkins

Wooden dowel

Decorative stickers

The Dirty Napkin Trick

Magic can have the most powerful effect when people are not expecting it. Here's a trick you could do during a meal. Sarah has this trick well under control. When the person opposite her has sat down and spread his paper napkin on his knee, she asks him for the napkin. She gives the excuse that she has noticed some tiny stains on it. To do the trick she tears off pieces from the centre of the napkin, explaining each time that, "this one's gravy, this one's ketchup", and so on. Finally she opens the napkin out to show that it is whole – without any bits torn out of it. This trick is a real reputation maker. Try it yourself.

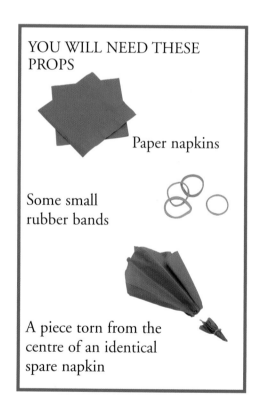

YOU WILL NEED THESE PROPS

Paper napkins

Some small rubber bands

A piece torn from the centre of an identical spare napkin

Tip
Don't use your own napkin for the secret torn piece, as someone might ask to see it afterwards. When you tear off the pieces, remove the rubber band with one of them (see step 6).

1 Secretly, under the table, attach the torn piece of napkin to the inside of your left thumb with the rubber band, so that it is hidden in your hand.

2 Borrow a napkin from another diner. No one will notice the torn piece as you reach across the table to take the napkin.

3 Spread the napkin over your left hand and point to the "stains" as you push the centre of the napkin into your hand.

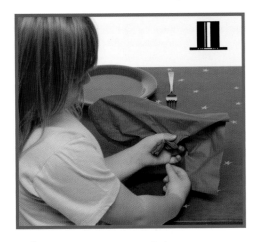

4 The real centre, and the torn centre, are side by side. Here we can see under Sarah's napkin, but don't let anyone else see what is happening.

5 Take both the centres into your right hand. Turn them upside down and put them back into your left hand. Pull up only the torn piece.

6 Tear off pieces, saying they are stained, and put them in your pocket. Remove the rubber band with one of the pieces.

7 Really, you are tearing pieces from the extra piece in your hand. It will look as if you are tearing them from the centre of the napkin.

8 When it looks like you have thoroughly spoilt the napkin, calmly open out the real napkin to the amazement of everyone at the table.

Money from Nowhere!

How about this for a trick? You are holding your empty top hat in one hand, then, with the other hand, you reach up and pluck a gold coin out of the air and drop it into your hat. Then you find another in the air, then another and another. Aribibia is finding coins all over the place, even behind people's ears! Finally he tips his hat onto the table and out pours a shower of golden coins. There are enough coins to hand out to friends after the show. When you do this trick, you will use a specially prepared coin, so make sure you do not give it away but keep it safely for next time.

Tip

For your special coin, to save it melting, carefully take the chocolate out of the foil and make it vanish, in your mouth! Replace it with a disc of cardboard and you can use the coin over and over again.

YOU WILL NEED THESE PROPS

Sticking plaster tape

Scissors

Chocolate money

Your top hat, with the flap

1 Before you start the trick, fix about 4 cm of sticking plaster to one side of your special coin, leaving about 2 cm hanging free.

2 Load one side of your hat flap with chocolate money. With the flap over the money, you can show your audience that the hat is "empty".

3 Hold the coin between your finger and thumb with the plaster stuck to your second and third fingers. Keep the back of your hand to the audience.

4 Hold your hand over the hat, and let the coin go. It will fall behind your fingers, but the audience will believe it has fallen into the hat.

5 Flick the coin up again, and catch it with your thumb. You've caught a coin from the air! Drop it into the hat. Repeat this action several times.

6 Shake the hat to rattle the coins that are already in it. The audience will be convinced that you have caught a hatful of coins from thin air.

7 Finally pour the coins onto the table to show just how many you have collected from thin air.

201

Magic Wands

It always looks good, in your show, to wave your wand whenever you wish the "magic" to happen. Nhat Han has also discovered some tricks that use the wand itself. She can make the wand "magnetic"; it will cling to her hand with, apparently, nothing holding it in place. She can, or so it appears, push the wand right into her leg and it doesn't hurt her. She can also make her wand stiff one minute and bendy the next. How does she do that?

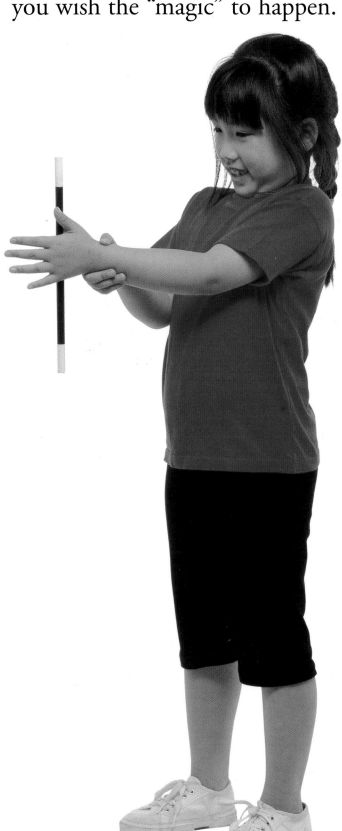

YOU WILL NEED THESE PROPS

Your wand, or a pencil

White paper

Scissors

Glue stick

Magnetic Wand

1 If you are holding a wand and you open your hand, it falls to the floor. Oh, dear!

2 But if you are a magician, like Nhat Han, it will stay in your hand all by itself.

3 Look on the other side of her hand. Can you see her secret? Try it yourself.

Painless Wand

1 Nhat Han rolls up a piece of white paper and glues it to make a tube the same size as the tip of her wand.

2 Nhat Han has pushed the wand right into her leg! But it did not seem to hurt! How did she do that?

3 She hid the lower wand tip in her hand and pushed the paper tube down the wand with her other hand.

Wobbly Wand

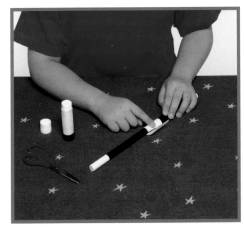

1 Nhat Han is trying to bend her wand. It is definitely stiff.

2 Next, she holds it loosely between finger and thumb, about one third of the way down. When she moves it from side to side, it looks wobbly.

The Coin Fold

Tricks with money always get the audience's attention, especially if you make the money disappear and it belongs to someone in the audience! Alexander finds that the coin fold shown here is a very useful method for helping to make a coin vanish easily. But he had to practise hard to perfect his technique, especially making the coin reappear from Michelle's ear.

YOU WILL NEED THESE PROPS

Coin

Paper

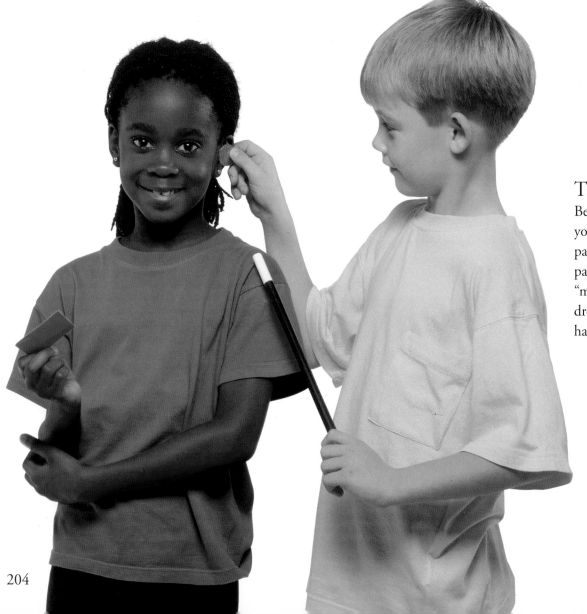

Tip

Because the audience sees you wrap the coin in the paper, their eyes stay on the paper packet. This "misdirection" allows you to drop the coin into your hand.

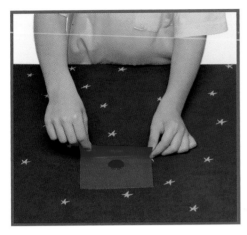

1 Place the coin in the middle of the paper and fold about one-third of the paper over it.

2 Press this down. It helps if you leave a coin-shaped impression in the paper.

3 Turn the paper and coin over, carefully, holding the coin in the fold of the paper, as Alexander is doing here.

4 Fold over about one-third from one side.

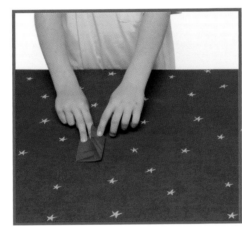

5 Then fold over about the same from the other side, so that the folds overlap.

6 Now fold the flap at the top over the other folds. Put the package in your left hand and hold a corner of the flap with your left thumb.

7 Gently lift the package, so that the coin slides out of the secret gap and stays hidden in your hand. Hold it with your second and third fingers.

8 Now you can tear up the package in front of the audience. Or you can hand it to a friend to hold, and pretend to find the coin in her ear.

Cutting Coins

Here is a routine that uses the coin fold principle demonstrated in the previous trick, some misdirection and a technique called "sleeving" the coin. The trick is a bit complicated to do, and might need a lot of practice. But if you can do this trick successfully, everyone will be convinced that you really *are* a magician. You will need to wear a jacket, blazer or similar clothing, with an inside breast pocket. Look at the pictures carefully. Notice in particular how Lucy uses her eyes to draw the audience's attention to exactly where she wants them to look, while she is doing the secret move somewhere else.

Tip

Put the scissors in your breast pocket before you start the routine. Place them point down. If you borrow the coin, you could get the lender to sign it with a felt-tipped pen, or remember the date on the coin. This will prove that you are using only one coin.

All the time you are performing the trick, keep your eyes on the packet to misdirect your audience.

YOU WILL NEED THESE PROPS

Coin

Pad of paper

Blunt-ended scissors

Jacket with inside breast pocket

1 Borrow a coin and do the coin fold as described in Steps 1 to 7 in the previous trick. Keep the coin hidden in your right hand.

2 Reach into your breast pocket for the scissors, but first drop the coin into your sleeve. Keep your arm bent up, so the coin stays near the elbow.

3 Bring out the scissors and cut the packet into little pieces. The coin has vanished! (You know it is in your sleeve by your elbow.)

4 Make up another little packet, keeping your arm with the coin bent. The audience can see that your hands, and the paper, are empty.

5 Rattle the packet and listen to it. Look as if you can hear a coin in there. This misdirects the audience while you drop your left hand naturally to your side. Catch the coin with your fingers as it slides out of your sleeve.

6 Keeping the coin hidden, bring both hands together and quickly tear open the paper packet. The coin that was hidden in your fingers seems to come out of the empty packet.

207

Middle House Mouse

This trick is loosely based on what's probably the oldest magic trick in the world, the "cups and balls", which is over 2000 years old. When Wura performs the trick using fluffy mice, she tells a story about a mouse who only ever wanted to live in a middle house, never at the end of a row.

Tip

You do not have to use mice. Look in the shops for four identical novelty animals that fit in your cups or you could even make your own.

The beakers or cups need to be of flexible plastic, not china or metal.

To make the bases for your animals, draw around a beaker onto the cardboard. Ask a grown-up to cut out the circle so that it is just a little *smaller* than the mouth of the beaker.

Never ever show more than one mouse at one time. The audience must believe that there is only one.

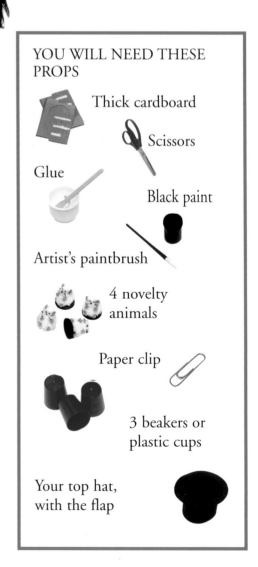

YOU WILL NEED THESE PROPS

Thick cardboard

Scissors

Glue

Black paint

Artist's paintbrush

4 novelty animals

Paper clip

3 beakers or plastic cups

Your top hat, with the flap

1 Ask a grown-up to cut out three circles to just fit inside a beaker. Paint them black. Leave to dry, then glue the circles onto the three mice.

2 Unbend the paper clip to make a hook at each end. Push one end into the fourth mouse. Hook it to your back before starting the trick.

3 Practise lifting up a beaker with a mouse inside. If you squeeze the cup when you lift it, the mouse stays in the cup and seems to "disappear".

4 Now for the performance. Arrange three beakers, each with a mouse hidden inside, in a line. Show the audience only the middle mouse.

5 Squeeze the two end beakers gently as you lift them (to hold the mice inside) to show they are "empty".

6 Swap the two end beakers with the middle one. Then lift the new middle beaker to show that the mouse has magically jumped back.

7 Swap the beakers again. Take the mouse from the end cup, and put it in your top hat. Lift the middle cup. The mouse has "jumped" back again!

8 Repeat until all the mice are in the hat, then show that the hat is also "empty". The audience will see where the mouse is when you turn round!

Postman's Wand

Gerald is demonstrating a really smart trick he has learnt. He puts his wand into an envelope, ready to post it. Then he performs a little magic, and "alakazam", the wand disappears from the envelope and then it reappears in a different envelope on the other side of the room.

Tips

Find some large envelopes that fit your wand, in different colours if possible or decorate them differently.

Make sure the envelopes stay in view at all times. Prop them up against the backs of two chairs if necessary.

Before you put the wand into the envelope, tap the chairs or tables with the wand. This proves that the wand is solid without your actually having to say so, which would seem suspicious.

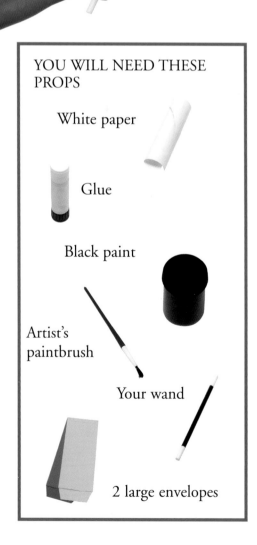

YOU WILL NEED THESE PROPS

White paper

Glue

Black paint

Artist's paintbrush

Your wand

2 large envelopes

1 Roll up some paper and glue it to make a hollow paper wand. Paint it to look like a real wand. When the paint is dry, slide it over the real wand.

2 Show your audience the two empty envelopes and place them apart on two tables or chairs.

3 Put the wand into one envelope. Shake your head and take it out, secretly letting the real wand slide out of the paper one into the envelope.

4 Put the paper wand into the other envelope, saying, "I prefer it in this one". Now the trick is done, but the audience thinks it has just started.

5 So now it is all acting. Make a magical "swapping over" sign with your arms.

6 The audience saw you put the wand in the second envelope yet you can prove it is now empty by scrunching it up into a ball.

7 With a grand gesture, open up the first envelope to reveal your real wand, which has magically travelled through the air. Magician, take a bow.

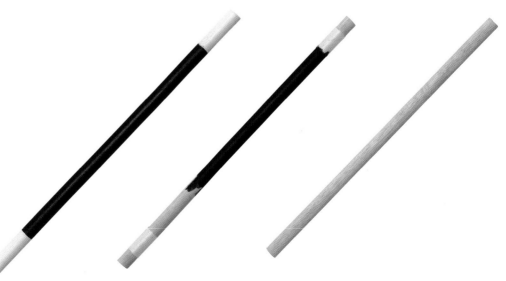

211

Back-flip Card

When people know you do magic, they will often ask to see a card trick. The trouble is, many card tricks involve complicated, finger-twisting moves. But try this: if you can put a pack of cards behind your back, turn the whole pack over and then turn just the top card over, you can do this trick. It is that easy. You have to have a reason for putting the cards behind your back, so explain that anyone can do a card trick when they can see the cards, but it takes a *real* magician to do it behind their back. Here, Michelle tries the trick out on Alexander.

Tip
When someone has chosen a card, ask them to show it to someone else (not you!). This helps to avoid them forgetting which card they chose, which would spoil the trick.

YOU WILL NEED THESE PROPS

Pack of cards

1 Shuffle the cards, then hold them like a fan, face-down in your hand. Ask a friend to take a card and remember it, but not to let you see it.

2 While talking about doing tricks behind your back, put the pack behind your back and turn it over. Pick off the top card.

3 Turn this card over and put it back on top of the pack. Do this quite quickly. Then bring the cards to the front again.

4 Hold the cards as a pack. All the cards are face up except the top one. Ask your friend to slide his card into the pack; keep the pack closed.

5 Put the pack behind your back again and pick off the top card.

6 Turn over the top card and put it back on the pack. Then turn the whole pack over while you say you are trying to find your friend's card.

7 Bring the pack to the front again and spread them out. Hocus-pocus! One card is face up, and yes – it is the very card that was chosen!

Coin Through Hand

An impromptu trick is one that you can do anywhere with no preparation or "props". All you need for this impromptu trick is your hands and a coin, which you can borrow. It is also very easy to do and is the first coin trick real magicians usually learn. You can really "act" this one. The audience, at first, think they have caught you out, so they are even more surprised when the coin really does end up in your fist. Michael shows us how to do it.

YOU WILL NEED THESE PROPS

Coin

Tip
Use a medium to large coin, if possible. Small, light coins sometimes stick to your fingers and do not drop when you want them to.

1 Hold the coin above your left fist, as shown, and announce, "I'm going to push this coin through the back of my hand".

2 As you push the coin down, it slides up, out of sight behind your fingers. "There, it's gone through", you can say.

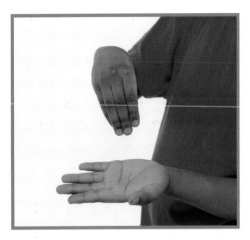

3 Open your fist and say, "Whoops! It must have got stuck, halfway". The audience, though, think they know where it is.

4 "I'll try again", you say as you do the sneaky bit. The sneaky bit is that, as you turn your left hand back over into a fist, your thumb almost brushes against the tips of the fingers holding the coin. Just at this point you let the coin slip out of your fingers, and you catch it in your left hand, which you make into a fist.

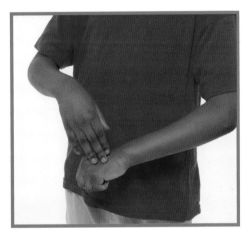

5 It all happens so quickly the audience believe it is still hidden behind your fingers, and you say, "I'll give it a harder push this time".

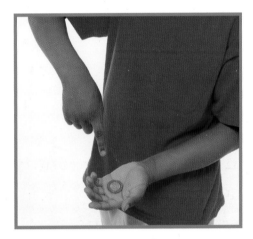

6 Now slowly turn your fist over and open it up. "Ah, there it is!"

Purple Hanky, Red Hanky

People in the audience love to come up and help during a show. For this trick, two assistants are needed. Nicola cleverly chose Scott, who was wearing a purple T-shirt, to hold the wrapped purple silk hanky, and Tope, who was wearing red, to hold the wrapped red silk hanky. Scott and Tope never let go of their parcels, but Nicola makes them keep changing sides. A wave of her wand and, "Hey presto", the hankies have changed places. Now, that *is* magic! How is it done? Well, the newspapers are not as ordinary as they seem.

Tips

If you choose volunteers who are wearing the same colours as your silk handkerchiefs, it is easier for the audience to follow the trick and for you to remember where the different silks are all the time.

When you tear open the parcel at the end of the trick, take care not to tear too deeply or you will expose the wrong silk.

YOU WILL NEED THESE PROPS

2 pairs of silk hankies in contrasting colours, such as red and purple

Newspaper

Glue stick

Sticky tape

Your wand

1 Before the show, lay out a silk handkerchief on a sheet of newspaper and spread glue round it (not on it!) with the glue stick.

2 Stick a second sheet on top. Do the same with a silk in the other colour. Make a secret mark on the papers, so you know which is which.

3 Fold up the sheets of newspapers and put them on your table, with your wand and the sticky tape. Show the audience the remaining two silks.

4 Wrap the red silk in the paper which has the purple one hidden inside, and make a rough ball shape.

5 Use sticky tape to hold the parcel together. Now wrap the purple silk in the paper with the red one inside, and hold it together with sticky tape.

6 Ask for two volunteers. Give the wrapped red silk to someone wearing red, and the wrapped purple silk to someone in purple.

7 Ask your volunteers to swap places while holding onto their parcels. Wave your wand in the air to make the magic work.

8 Tear open the outer layer of the "purple" parcel. Instead of a purple silk, you pull out a red one! And from the "red" you pull out a purple silk.

X-ray Wand and Ringing Up

Here are two special tricks using magic wands, but with a difference. The second trick uses your wooden wand, but the first one uses a hollow wand. Carl has made a hollow wand by rolling up a sheet of paper and painting it to look like a real one. The X-ray Wand routine is perfect for when you are showing a trick to just one friend, because you actually teach them how to do it. They will be amazed to see a hole right through their hand. Ringing Up is great fun because you can use a ring that you have borrowed from someone in the audience. People always enjoy seeing their own things behaving in strange magical ways.

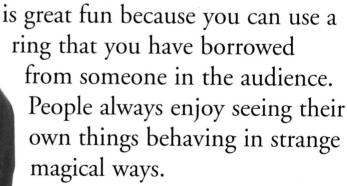

YOU WILL NEED THESE PROPS

White paper

Glue stick

Black paint

Artist's paintbrush

Black thread

Reusable sticky tac

Safety pin

Your wand

Ring

X-ray Wand

1 Roll and glue a sheet of paper to form a tube. Then paint it to look like a wand.

2 Hold the paper wand up to your eye and look through it, keeping both eyes open.

3 Place your other hand, open flat, about halfway along it, beside the wand.

4 Now you will see a hole right through your hand!

Ringing Up

1 Attach a black thread to your wand with sticky tac. Tie the thread to a safety pin; fix this to your waist. Put a ring over the wand to rest on your fist.

2 Wriggle your other fingers as you move the wand slightly away from yourself – the ring starts to rise. How?

3 As you move the wand forwards, the thread attached to the top of your trousers and to the wand moves higher, pushing the ring up the wand.

Time-bomb Escape

How would you like to do a really dangerous and "death-defying" trick to add drama and suspense to your show? Imagine, then, being tied up in a time-bomb and escaping with only seconds to spare. You could pretend to be like Houdini, who was one of the greatest magicians and escapologists of all time. Before you start, ask a grown-up to

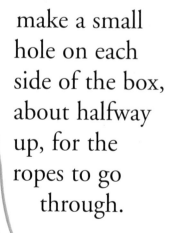

make a small hole on each side of the box, about halfway up, for the ropes to go through.

Tips

Decorate your box to make it look really dangerous!

Once you are shut in the box, get the audience to count down from 30 to 1 and then, if you have not escaped, to shout "Bang".

With practice, you will find you can free yourself from the ropes in only a few seconds, but do not jump out too early. The effect is much more dramatic if you leave it until there are only two or three seconds to spare!

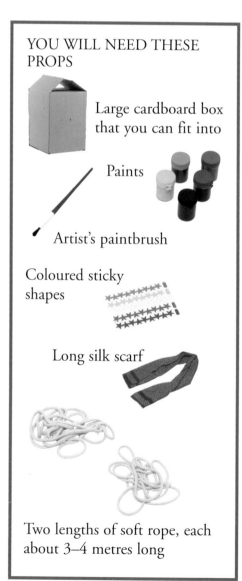

YOU WILL NEED THESE PROPS

Large cardboard box that you can fit into

Paints

Artist's paintbrush

Coloured sticky shapes

Long silk scarf

Two lengths of soft rope, each about 3–4 metres long

1 Ask one of your assistants to tie your hands with the scarf. Tie the scarf round one wrist, then the other next to it, firmly, but not *too* tightly.

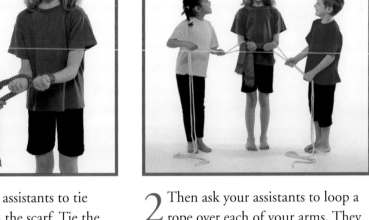

2 Then ask your assistants to loop a rope over each of your arms. They must hold on firmly to the ends of the ropes, not letting go until the trick is completed. You will be trapped!

3 Climb into the box with an assistant standing guard on each side. Ask them to push the free ends of the ropes out through the small holes in the sides of the box, and then keep hold of them.

4 Squat down inside the box and tell your assistants to close the flaps. Now they can start the countdown with the audience: 30, 29, 28…

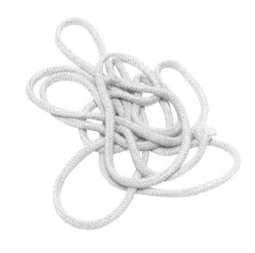

5 Even though you are tied up, you will be able to work the rope free. Pull a loop of the rope down the inside of your wrist under the silk scarf.

6 Push the loop back over your hand and let it slide up the back of your wrist. That hand is free. Now do the other one.

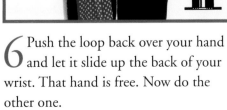

7 With only a few seconds of the countdown to spare, jump up like a jack-in-the-box, holding your arms in the air to show they are free.

I Can Grow Things

Introduction

Gardens and gardeners come in many
shapes and sizes. You can be a
gardener too, whether you live
on a farm with a large
garden or in an
apartment with
some space
on a windowsill
for a few plants.

Pot marigolds

Growing things takes
time and patience, but the
rewards are worth waiting for.
There are lots of other things
for you to be getting on with
while your seeds are germinating
under the soil. Once you see the first green shoots appear
you will know that a plant really is going to grow and you
are already a gardener!

In this chapter we
show you how to
grow lots of different
plants yourself, with perhaps just a little help
from a grown-up.

There are plants
that grow very
fast and produce something
to eat, like mustard and cress.

Strawberries

Some plants take longer to grow
but give you special treats, like strawberries. Other plants
are grown just for fun, like vegetable tops and a coconut
head. So, whether you choose to grow giant sunflowers
that take all summer, or
sprouting seeds for your
salad that are ready in
just a few days, you will
find out all you need to
know by following what
the children are doing in
the pictures.

Different plants grow,
then flower and die with the seasons.

Vegetable tops

Daffodils like the crisp, cold springtime sunshine while nasturtiums thrive in the baking hot summer sun, needing no shade and very little water. Some plants live through the winter, growing new flowers each summer. Others live only for one season but make seeds that will grow into new plants the following year. Houseplants usually come from parts of the world where the weather is warmer all year round, but they grow very happily indoors in countries with cooler climates.

How Plants Begin to Grow

Plants start growing in many different ways and it is important to know how to treat each type. Look at the list below to find out how plants can be grown.

Seeds

A seed needs water to soften its outer shell, and then the new plant sends a root downwards into the soil and a stem upwards, towards the light. The tiniest seeds just need to be scattered on top of the soil, but the larger ones have to be buried. Usually seeds are planted as deep as they are *Seeds* thick. So measure a seed between your fingers and you will know how deep it has to go into the soil in order to grow properly.

Bulbs, corms and tubers

Bulbs

Tubers

Corms

These are thick, fleshy and roundish in shape. A bulb looks like an onion – in fact if you planted an onion it would grow leaves and flowers! They all produce new plants which will grow in the right conditions. Some need icy cold winters underground and others should only be planted when the weather gets warmer. Daffodils grow from bulbs, begonias from corms and dahlias from tubers.

Grow a new plant from a stem cutting

Cuttings

Some plants need very special conditions to make their seeds grow, but you can still grow some new plants from cuttings. Take a piece of the healthy full-grown plant, and stand it in water or compost in a warm place. It will grow roots from its stem and you will soon have a strong little plant. Some plants can be grown from leaf or root cuttings as well.

Plantlets

Some fully-grown plants send out long runners which grow miniature plants at their ends. These send down roots of their own if they rest on the soil, and eventually the runners will die back to leave a separate new plant. Strawberries and spider plants grow in this way.

Grow a new plant from plantlets

Caring for Your Plants

Your seeds, bulbs, cuttings and plantlets will only grow into healthy adult plants if you look after them carefully. This doesn't need to take a lot of time, but you do need to remember to look at them every few days to check that they are doing well.

Watering

Watering your plants is a lot of fun, but if you give them too much they will rot and die. Try to keep the soil damp but not wet. When you press it with your finger, you should be able to feel the moisture without a little pool of water forming. If your plants do dry out, stand their pots in a saucer or bowl of water rather than pour on water

Test the soil to see if it needs more water

If the soil is dry, stand the pot in a bowl of water

from above. This way the soil will gradually soak up water to feed the thirsty roots.

Weeds

If you do your gardening outdoors, you may find that other little plants also begin to grow where you haven't planted any seeds. Ask a grown-up to show you what weeds look like, and try to keep your garden weed-free. It seems cruel to pull out healthy little plants, but if you leave them they will spread very quickly and stop your plants from getting the light and moisture that they need to grow. So pull them up before they grow big enough to flower and make more seeds to grow more weeds.

Pests

These are creatures that we don't want around us, and in the garden they include greenfly, caterpillars, snails and slugs. They love eating juicy new plants but luckily there are some other creatures that like eating them. Ladybirds love greenfly, but they can't always eat them up quickly enough so you may have to do something. Try adding a small amount of washing-up soap to a spray bottle filled with water and then use it to spray the greenfly on your plants. If you have a problem with slugs and snails, you can sprinkle ashes or sand around your lettuces as they don't like the feeling of sliding over it. Caterpillars need to be removed by hand and – if you don't mind doing it – just drop them into a jar of water. Otherwise, set them free somewhere far away from your precious plants.

Spray a plant with soapy water to get rid of greenfly

Important!

Remember that even the most expert gardeners sometimes have failures, when plants don't grow, or pests become a big problem. If this happens to you, try not to feel discouraged. The best thing to do is to try something new so that you always have some gardening on the go!

Latin Names

Every plant has a special Latin name that tells you exactly what it is. Just like we have our Christian names and surnames, a plant has a family name first and its own name second. The names are often difficult to say, but if you take a few letters at a time you will be able to join them up and say something in Latin. When they are printed in a book, Latin names appear in italics, like this: *Helianthus debilis*. *Helianthus* is the family name for sunflowers, and *debilis* is the special name given to a small, or dwarf, type of sunflower.

Glossary

Here are some special gardening words that you may not know but will see mentioned in the projects.

Alpine A rock garden plant.
Annual A plant that completes its life cycle in one year. It starts by growing from a seed and finishes by making new seeds.
Compost A special soil mixture or rotted-down garden and kitchen waste that feeds the plants so they grow well.
Crocks Broken pieces of clay flowerpot. They are used in the bottom of pots to help with drainage.
Cutting A piece of plant (leaf, stem or root) which can be used to grow a new plant.
Germination The first stage of growth from seed to plant.
Node A stem joint, where new stems and leaves grow.
Mulch A layer of chopped up leaves, bark or other plant matter. It is spread on top of the soil to stop it drying out and to prevent weeds from growing.
Propagating Growing new plants by different methods, including taking cuttings.
Runner A creeping stem which grows roots and produces new plants.

Mulches stop the soil drying out so quickly

New umbrella plants are grown from cuttings

Spider plants grow runners

227

Finding What You Need

A garden centre can be very large and confusing when you only need a few small things to start you off. Here is a basic list of useful gardening materials and tools. You will be able to get some of the equipment mentioned here from toy shops, too, such as a small plastic watering can, a scoop to use as a trowel and a sieve, which are often sold for playing with in sandpits.

Trowel You will need a small trowel for filling flowerpots with compost and for digging holes in the garden.

Watering can A can with a sprinkler will be best for gentle watering. Remember that water is very heavy to carry, so choose the size of can that you will be able to lift easily when it is full.

Sieve This is useful for sprinkling a very fine layer of compost over your newly-sown seeds.

Flowerpots These should always have a

drainage hole in the bottom. They come in lots of different sizes, made from either clay or plastic, and they usually have matching saucers to stop drips. You can decorate clay pots at home or buy plastic ones in lots of fun colours. Don't forget to collect some pretty outer containers too. Clay pots need a layer of crocks or pebbles adding to them before the compost. This helps them to drain better after watering.

Peat pots These are special types of flowerpots which are usually used for planting seeds. When the new plant has started to grow the plant and its pot can be planted in a larger flowerpot. The peat pot will gradually dissolve in the compost.

Seed trays These are useful for planting lots of little seeds or for standing pots of seeds in. You can also use foil dishes used for freezing food.

Seed tray

Plastic flowerpots

Foil dish

Compost

Plastic bags

Plant labels

Watering

Pen

Plant food

Hairpins

Peat pots

Sieve

Compost Specially prepared soils that we buy in bags are called composts. There are lots of different mixtures that suit some types of plant better than others. Seed and cutting compost will give you the best chance of success with new plants. Houseplant compost is useful for indoor gardeners. Cactus compost is good for succulents. Any all-purpose compost is good for general growing, and it comes in bags of all sizes.

Plant food Some plants need more "food" than they can get from compost alone while they are growing. Always ask a grown-up to help you measure out the correct amount of special plant food, following the instructions on the bottle or packet.

Crocks and pebbles These are used to provide better drainage in the bottom of clay pots. You can also sprinkle a layer of pebbles or gravel on top of the compost. This both looks nice and is good for the plants as it helps to keep the soil moist.

Canes and string Some plants grow tall and their stems need to be supported to stop them bending or breaking.

Hairpins These are used to pin baby plantlets growing on the end of runners into compost so that they form roots.

Plant labels and pen Always label your plants so you can remember what you are growing in different pots.

Seeds, bulbs etc There are usually more than you need in a packet, so before buying any ask grown-up gardeners, like your parents, grandparents or neighbours, whether they can spare you a few of their left-over seeds or bulbs. Gardeners always like to share things.

Plastic flowerpots

Plant containers

Trowels

Watering can

Safety scissors

Pebbles

Crocks

String

Seeds and bulbs

Canes

A Sunflower Race

You have to look up to see a sunflower, because they are the tallest and the biggest flowers that we grow in our gardens. It's great fun to have a sunflower race with your friends or family. Roxy and Dominic are having a sunflower race. Follow the step-by-step photographs to see who won.

Tasty pickings

The flower centres of sunflowers are sometimes as large as dinner plates and packed with tasty seeds. These seeds can be eaten raw once the husks have been removed, or the whole flowerhead can be dried and hung out to feed the birds in winter. In hot countries you can see whole fields of huge sunflowers that are grown to make cooking oil and margarine.

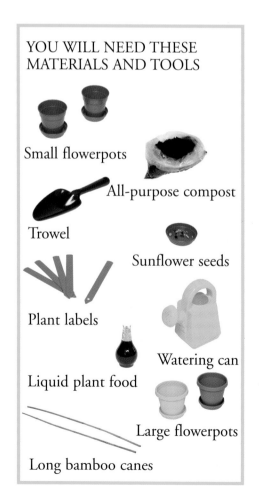

YOU WILL NEED THESE MATERIALS AND TOOLS

Small flowerpots

All-purpose compost

Trowel

Sunflower seeds

Plant labels

Watering can

Liquid plant food

Large flowerpots

Long bamboo canes

1 Fill some pots with compost and press in the sunflower seeds.

2 Water the pots and cover them with black plastic, or put them in a dark place to germinate.

Size is Not Everything

If you really love sunflowers but have no space to grow the very tall ones, don't worry – you can grow the smaller types. Buy a packet of sunflower seed called *Helianthus debilis.* Sow the seeds into peat pots and then move them into medium-sized flowerpots or a space in the garden, if you have one. They will grow about 80 cm (2ft 8 in) tall, and are just as beautiful.

3 When the seeds germinate and you can see a bit of green, move the pots into the light.

4 When the seedlings are big enough to handle, they can be moved into bigger pots. To help them grow strong and tall you will need to give them a liquid feed once a week. Ask a grown-up to help you with this.

Above: As the plants grow you will need to move them into even larger pots or plant them in the garden. They will need canes to support them.

Some of the plants will be bigger than you are. Measure each one to find the winner of the great sunflower race. This one is a dead heat!

Juicy Strawberries

Strawberry plants have very pretty pink or white flowers with yellow centres, and when the petals drop the fruits begin to grow. They are green at first and then white. As they get bigger and juicier, and ripen in the sun they gradually turn a shiny bright red. If you can bear to wait you will find that the riper they get, the sweeter they taste.

How do baby strawberry plants grow?

Strawberry plants send out long thin stems called runners and baby plants form at their ends. They are fed by the root system of the parent plant through the runner. But if these babies come to rest on soil, they put down roots of their own and no longer need the parent plant to keep them alive. Tania is going to start off some baby strawberry plants and grow herself a mouthwatering treat.

Below: Delicious juicy strawberries – well worth waiting for.

YOU WILL NEED THESE
MATERIALS AND TOOLS

Small flowerpots
and saucers

Trowel

Potting compost

Strawberry plant
with runners

Hairpin for each
baby plant.

Watering can   Safety scissors

1 Fill the small flowerpots with potting compost and gently firm it down.

2 Place your pots around the parent plant so that a baby plant rests in each of the pots. Push a hairpin into the compost over the runner.

Cascading Strawberries

If you only have a small space for growing your fruits, a strawberry pot is useful and pretty. It is a tall pot with little "balconies" all the way around it. The idea is to fill the whole pot with compost and plant a small strawberry baby in each of the openings. Water each one and plant the biggest strawberry plant in the top of the pot. When the plants begin to grow they will cover the pot and strawberries will hang down in the sun to ripen.

3 Water all the pots. Remember to check the compost each day to be sure it never gets too dry.

4 When the plants have rooted you will see tiny new leaves beginning to sprout.

5 If the baby plants feel firm in the compost, you can now cut the runners.

6 As your plant grows it will need more space, either in the garden or a larger pot.

7 Remember to water your strawberry plant regularly. If it's kept too dry, the fruit will shrivel.

Coconut Head

This coconut head looks so funny that you'll have to be careful who you show it to – everyone will want one! They are so easy to do, and as the grass grows you will be able to change the hair-style of your coconut head. You could also try sowing mustard and cress for a really curly hair-style. Follow the method shown by Dominic and Alex.

Nuts about hair

You can buy grass seed in small amounts from most hardware stores or garden centres, and just 50 g (2 oz) will grow a really good "head of hair" for your coconut. You will have to ask a grown-up to saw or break the top off your coconut, because the shells are really hard. If you haven't eaten fresh coconut before or drunk coconut milk, try some – it's really tasty! Put some out for the birds as a treat.

YOU WILL NEED THESE
MATERIALS AND TOOLS

Fresh coconut

Flowerpot

Marker pen

Trowel

Compost

Grass seed

Soil sieve

Watering can

Black plastic bag

1 Ask a grown-up to take the top off your coconut. Pour out the milk and ask someone to help you remove the flesh – it's quite difficult.

2 Stand the coconut shell in a flower-pot to stop it falling over, and draw a face on it with a chunky marker pen.

3 Fill your coconut with compost, pressing it down gently.

4 Scatter grass seed thickly over the top of the compost.

5 Sieve a thin layer of compost over to cover all the seed. Press down gently again.

6 Water and cover with a black plastic bag, or put in a dark place until the seeds have begun to grow.

7 When green shoots appear, stand the coconut in the light and water when it looks dry. When the grass has grown over the rim of the coconut, it is ready for its first haircut.

Above: Before and after! If you keep snipping the grass as it grows, it will get thicker and thicker!

Jolly Geraniums

Geraniums are lovely, bright flowering plants that live outside in the sunny weather. In the winter they can be brought inside to live on a sunny windowsill. Their flowers are either red, white or pink and they have pretty shaped leaves – some of them are scented. Rub a leaf between your fingers to discover their surprising smells of rose, lemon, pineapple or peppermint!

Taking a cutting

The best way to grow your very own geranium plant is to find somebody who owns a nice bushy geranium, and ask them to take a cutting for you. Tania is going to start a plant from a cutting. Just follow the step-by-step instructions, and you will be able to grow one too.

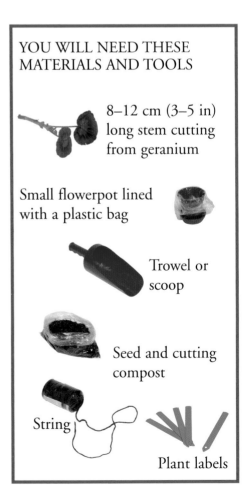

YOU WILL NEED THESE MATERIALS AND TOOLS

8–12 cm (3–5 in) long stem cutting from geranium

Small flowerpot lined with a plastic bag

Trowel or scoop

Seed and cutting compost

String

Plant labels

1 Ask a grown-up to take a cutting from a non-flowering shoot of a big geranium plant. Cut the stem just below a node or leaf joint.

2 Take off all leaves except for the small ones at the top.

3 Line a small pot with a plastic bag and fill with moist (but not wet) compost. Seed and cutting compost is the best type to use.

4 Make a hole in the compost for your cutting with a finger. Put the cutting in the hole. Press the compost down gently around the cutting to hold it in place.

5 Lift the edges of the plastic bag, gather it up and tie it around the stem of the cutting with string. Take care not to damage the stem by tying it too tightly.

6 Fold the top of the bag back down over the pot, write a label for your plant and place your pot on a light, but not too sunny, windowsill. After ten days your cutting should have rooted. When it has grown new leaves, lift up the plastic bag and you will see new roots in the compost. You can now remove the bag and plant the geranium in a larger pot.

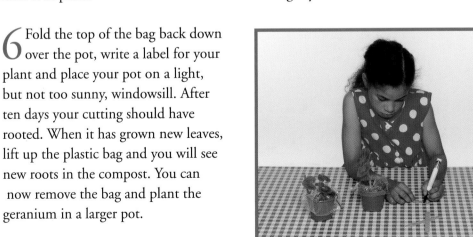

Above: What an achievement. Your very own plant from a cutting.

Crazy-Shaped Mustard and Cress

Once you have learned how to grow mustard and cress, you can make all sorts of shapes and patterns with your plants. Try animals and faces, or even your own name. Mustard and cress are fun to grow and delicious to eat in salads and sandwiches.

How to grow mustard and cress

Mustard and cress are two of the easiest and quickest plants you can grow. They don't need flowerpots or compost, just cotton wool and water. Sprinkle the seeds onto damp cotton wool and water them each day – as Alex and Reece are doing here. Within a week the little plants will be growing strongly and one week after that you can harvest them with a pair of scissors and then eat them. Your mustard and cress will taste just as good as the type you can buy from shops.

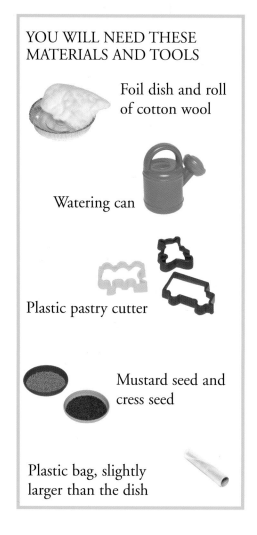

YOU WILL NEED THESE
MATERIALS AND TOOLS

Foil dish and roll of cotton wool

Watering can

Plastic pastry cutter

Mustard seed and cress seed

Plastic bag, slightly larger than the dish

1 Line a foil dish with a layer of cotton wool.

2 Pour on water, until all the cotton wool is damp.

3 Place the plastic pastry cutter in the centre of the dish.

4 Very carefully, scatter mustard seeds inside the cutter.

5 Now scatter the cress seeds all around the rest of the dish.

Mustard and Cress "Eggheads"

You can grow mustard and cress in eggshells. Save the shell from your boiled egg and line it with damp cotton wool. Sow the seed thickly and wait for your "egghead" to grow its hair. Use felt tipped pens to draw a happy face on the shell, and trim the mustard and cress into a nice "hair-style".

6 Place the dish in the plastic bag and put it in a dark place. Check the dish each day to see if the seeds have germinated. When they have, remove the plastic bag and place the dish on a light windowsill.

7 Add a little water to the dish each day – just enough to keep the cotton wool wet. When the plants are as tall as your little finger, you can cut the mustard and cress and put them in a salad or sandwich.

Creepy-Crawly Spider Plants

Spider plants are stripey and spikey and hang down like spiders' legs. They are happy to sit on an inside windowsill or you can put them in special hanging baskets. They will hang down from the ceiling, just like real spiders!

Happy houseplants

In warm countries spider plants grow outdoors, but in cooler places they are mainly grown as houseplants. All they need is some light and water. They will even let you know when they are thirsty, by turning a lighter shade of green. A happy spider plant sends out long stems that have baby plants on the ends, and these can be potted up and grown into new spider plants. Reece will show you how to grow new plants from spider plant runners. Just follow the step-by-step guide here.

YOU WILL NEED THESE MATERIALS AND TOOLS

Several small flowerpots and saucers

Trowel

Houseplant compost

Spider plant with babies

Hairpins

Watering can

Safety scissors

1 Fill the small flowerpots with compost.

2 Press the compost down using the base of another pot.

Other Plants with Babies

The common name of the *Tolmiea menziesii* is the piggyback plant, because new young plants form on the leaves of the parent plant. Just take the leaves with babies on and pin them onto the surface of a pot of compost, using a hairpin. Water and leave in a sunny place. The little plants will soon root and begin to grow. Then you can move them into their own pots.

3 Place the pots around the parent plant, so that a baby plant rests comfortably in each of the pots. Use the hairpins to hold the baby plants firmly in place.

4 Water all the plants. Remember to check the pots each day to make sure that they don't get too dry.

5 When the plants have rooted you will notice new leaves beginning to sprout. Now you can carefully cut the runners.

Right: Finally, the reward for all your care – a new spider plant.

243

Chocolate-Pot Plant

Can you believe your nose? This lovely plant smells exactly like chocolate! It is a very special sort of cosmos daisy that is bought as a small plant and, if it is kept out of the cold, it will flower again next year.

What a wonderful smell!
To make the smell of chocolate even stronger and more delicious, Dominic and Alex have used a special mulch to cover the soil. This mulch is made from cocoa shells after the cocoa beans have been removed to make chocolate. It has a lovely chocolate smell and is also good for the soil!

YOU WILL NEED THESE MATERIALS AND TOOLS

Large clay pot

Acrylic paint

Paintbrush

Crocks

Cosmos daisy (*Cosmos astrosanguineus*)

All-purpose compost

Trowel

Saucer filled with gravel

Cocoa-shell mulch

Watering can

Right: A chocolate-pot plant would be a lovely and unusual present for someone special – if you can bear to part with it.

1 Use a round paintbrush to paint coloured dots all around your flowerpot.

2 When the paint has dried, put some crocks in the bottom, so that the drainage hole does not clog up.

3 Remove your plant from its pot very carefully. If its roots have started to curl around inside the pot, gently loosen the roots as Alex is doing here.

4 Put the plant into the decorated pot and fill all around the roots with compost, pressing down the edges until the plant is firmly in position.

5 Cover the soil around the plant with a thick layer of cocoa-shell mulch.

6 Stand the pot on the saucer filled with gravel and water the plant thoroughly.

7 Press the flower petals gently between your fingers to release a delicious chocolate smell.

8 After all that hard work, and the tempting smells, a real chocolate was irresistible.

More Surprising Smells

A lemon balm plant will grow very quickly. Plant it in a medium-sized flowerpot in all-purpose compost. When you rub the leaves between your fingers, a lovely lemony smell is released. Another surprising plant is one of the sages, *Salvia elegans*. It has a mouthwatering smell of pineapple. There is a mint and a geranium that have a pineapple smell too.

Sprouting Seeds – Jam-Jar Salads

You won't need a garden, or even a windowsill to grow these delicious, crunchy salad sprouts. All you need is a jam jar with some air holes in the lid and some seeds and beans. What could be simpler?

Healthy harvest

If you go to a healthfood shop where they weigh out their own grains and pulses, you will be able to buy small amounts of all kinds of suitable seeds for sprouting. Aduki beans, mung beans, brown lentils, sunflower seeds, chickpeas, sesame seeds and alfalfa seeds are all easy sprouters. You will need to have a jam jar for each type, because every seed germinates at a different speed. A tablespoon of seeds or beans should make about 170 g (6 oz) sprouts. Laurence and Josie will show you exactly what to do.

YOU WILL NEED THESE
MATERIALS AND TOOLS

Jam jars

Sieve

Chickpeas, mung beans
and alfalfa seeds

Chinese-Style Beansprouts

The beansprouts that are sold in supermarkets are mung beans that have been germinated in water and kept in the dark. Try growing beansprouts in the same way as salad sprouts, but don't move them into the light. Change their water regularly, and when they look thick and juicy take them out and rinse in a sieve. The beansprouts can be used to make a Chinese stir-fry. Ask a grown-up to mix them up with slivers of carrot, peas, sweetcorn and a bit of oil. They only need to cook for 5 minutes. Add a dash of soy sauce for a tasty meal!

1 Wash some jam jars and their lids. You need a separate jar for each type of seed or bean you are using.

2 Ask a grown-up to help you make holes in the lids.

3 Put a tablespoonful of seeds or beans in each jar.

4 Rinse the seeds then cover them with lukewarm water.

5 Put the lids on the jars and turn them upside-down, so that most of the water drains away. Put the jars in a warm, dark place for three days.

6 Take them out every morning and evening, and give them a good rinse with cold water, draining each time as in Step 5. After three days, transfer the jars to a warm windowsill, and continue to rinse them out twice a day.

7 When the seeds have roots and leaf-tips they are ready to eat. Empty them into a sieve and rinse once more under the cold tap. A delicious crunchy salad snack grown in a jam jar!

Vegetable-Top Forest

Rosie and Tania are making up a miniature "forest" using several different vegetable tops. To make it look more realistic they have scattered compost and birdseed under their "trees" and grown some undergrowth. Dinosaurs or jungle animals could prowl about, hiding behind trees or sneaking through the long grass!

From roots to shoots

Beetroot, turnips, swedes, parsnips and carrots are all root vegetables because they grow under the soil. Unless we grow them ourselves, we never see what their leaves look like. But there is a way to grow the leaves from the vegetable tops that we usually throw away. Just stand the top of a root vegetable in a saucer of water, and leaves will begin to sprout from the top!

YOU WILL NEED THESE MATERIALS AND TOOLS

Selection of root vegetable tops

Foil tray

Gravel or small pebbles

Watering can

Compost

Birdseed or grass seed

1 Ask a grown-up to cut the tops off a variety of root vegetables for you. Vegetables like kohl-rabi, beetroot and turnips need half of the root, others just the top 3 cm (1 in).

2 Arrange the vegetable tops quite close together in a foil tray.

3 Surround them with gravel which will look like the forest floor.

4 Pour in 1 cm (½ in) of water and place on a sunny windowsill.

5 Add a little more water each day to make sure the roots don't dry out.

Weed Jungle

There is another type of forest that you can grow very quickly – a weed jungle. You have probably heard grown-ups complaining about how fast weeds grow in the garden. They grow even faster if you care for them! Half fill a shallow freezer tray with garden soil or compost. Use a spoon to dig up all sorts of small weeds, and plant them in your tray. Put the tray in a warm place and water when it is dry. Soon you will have a real jungle of leaves and flowers – a perfect home for small model jungle animals.

6 When the leaves are about 8 cm (3 in) tall, sprinkle the compost and birdseed or grass seed over the gravel, and water.

Left: Within a week you will have grown your own vegetable-top forest.

Upside-Down Umbrella Plants

Getting your feet wet

Umbrella plants love water. It is almost impossible to over-water them! This is because they belong to a family of water-loving reeds. They can grow to around 1.3 m (4 ft) tall and love sharing your bathroom where the air is always humid, and also warm in winter. Try growing them in a glass tank filled with water and pebbles.

Why are they called umbrella plants? Because their stems look like the skeletons of umbrellas. How do they make new plants? Upside-down! Have a look at how Joshua and Ilaira are propagating a new plant on the next page, then try it for yourself.

YOU WILL NEED THESE MATERIALS AND TOOLS

Umbrella plant
(Cyperus alternifolius)

Small glass tank

Gravel or small pebbles

Watering can

Safety scissors

Flat-bottomed glass dish

Flowerpot

Trowel   Houseplant compost

1 Take the plant out of its container and stand it in the glass tank, on a bed of gravel.

2 Fill all around the umbrella plant with gravel or stones, to the top of the compost.

3 Fill the tank with water to the top of the gravel. Umbrella plants grow naturally in shallow water at the river's edge, and enjoy having wet feet!

More Water-Loving Plants to Grow

If you have a patio or a garden, you could grow some water-loving plants in a small tub, or washing-up bowl. Some plants just float on the water, needing no stones or soil. The water violet is very easy to grow. If you know some-one with a garden pond, ask for some small bits from their plants.

4 To make new plants, cut off a flowerhead with 5 cm (2 in) of stem attached. The flowerheads need to be "mature". If they have brown tufts coming out from their centres they are just right for propagating.

5 Give the leaves a "haircut", so that they are about half their original length.

6 Fill the flat-bottomed dish with water and float the flowerheads upside-down on the surface.

7 When they have grown some roots, plant them in pots filled with houseplant compost.

Above: A brand new umbrella plant.

Lazy Summer Afternoons

Nasturtiums and pot marigolds are two plants for lazy gardeners! They need very little care – in fact they thrive and produce more flowers in poor-quality soil. So don't pamper them – they just don't like it. Follow the steps shown in the photographs to find out how it's done.

Pretty useful

Nasturtium flowers range from yellow to deep red, and marigold flowers are bright orange or yellow. Nasturtium flowers can be eaten raw. They have a peppery taste, and some supermarkets sell packets of the flowers that would turn a plain salad into a party dish. Marigolds are not eaten but they are used to make soothing skin lotions and healing ointments. Their petals were once used to colour cheeses, custards and cakes, too.

Neither of these plants likes to have its roots disturbed, so Dominic and Roxy are starting them off in little peat pots. The plants can be potted on in these because the peat will gradually dissolve into the new compost.

YOU WILL NEED THESE MATERIALS AND TOOLS

Peat pots

Trowel

Garden soil, or all-purpose compost

Nasturtium and pot marigold seeds

Plant labels

Seed tray

Watering can

Black plastic bag

Two large flowerpots and saucers

1 Fill the little peat pots with garden soil or compost.

2 Either sow one nasturtium or two marigold seeds in each pot, and gently firm them in.

3 Write a label for each kind of flower and put it in the pot.

4 Stand the pots in a seed tray and water them until the pots turn dark brown all over.

5 Cover the pots with a black plastic bag until the seeds have germinated and you can see green shoots. Then move them into a light place.

6 When the seeds are 5–8 cm (2–3 in) tall they can be planted in bigger pots. Break off each peat pot, and plant the pot with the seedlings.

7 Both marigolds and nasturtiums will produce seeds on their flower-heads when the petals have dropped. Let these dry and save them in labelled packets for next year's flower crop.

Above and right: The orange-yellow colour of marigold and nasturtium flowers are especially summery. You could transfer your plants to a windowbox for a pretty outdoor display of colour.

Index

Acknowledgements

The publishers would like to thank the following children for appearing in this book, and of course their parents: Josie and Lawrence Ainscombe, Clive Allen, Deborah Amoah, Rosie Anness, Michael Apeagyei, Tania and Joshua Ayshford, Venetia Barrett, Jason Bear, Emma Blue, Catherine Brown, Christopher Brown, Daniel Carlow, Alexander Clare, Rebecca Clee, Charlie Coulson, Brooke Crane, Dean Denning, Benjamin Ferguson, Aimee Fermor, Kirsty and Rebecca Fraser, Alice Granville, Liam and Lorenzo Green, Alexandra and Oliver Hall, Reece Harle, Jonathan Headon, Dominic Henry, Edward and Thomas Hogarth, Sasha Howarth, Gerald Ishiekwene, Saadia Jacobs, Stella-Rae James, Jade Jeffries, Aribibia Johnson, Carl Keating, Karina Kelly, Nicholas Lie, Sophie, Alex and Otis Lindblom-Smith, Chloe Lipton, Scott Longstaff, Ephram Lovemore, Jock Maitland, Gabriella and Izabella Malewska, Ilaira and Joshua Mallalieu, Alexander Martin-Simons, Hou Mau, Trevor Meechan, Jessica and Alice Moxley, Tania Murphy, Moriam Mustapha, Lucy Nightingale, Wura Odurinde, Abayomi Ojo, Michael Oloyede, Tope Oni, Alexander and Dominic Paneth, Patrice Picard, Alice Purton, Brandon Rayment, Aaron Singh, Antonino Sipiano, Justine Spiers, Nicola and Sarah Twiner, Nhat Han Vong, Rupert and Roxy Walton, George Wheeler, Claudius Wilson, Andreas Wiseman.

Contributors: Petra Boase, Stephanie Donaldson, Sarah Maxwell, Hugh Nightingale, Steve and Jane Parker, Michael Purton, Thomasina Smith, Sally Walton.